love
lives
here

A Story of Thriving in a
Transgender Family

Amanda Jetté Knox

VIKING

VIKING

an imprint of Penguin Canada, a division of Penguin Random House Canada Limited

Canada · USA · UK · Ireland · Australia · New Zealand · India · South Africa · China

First published 2019

www.penguinrandomhouse.ca

LIBRARY AND ARCHIVES CANADA CATALOGUING IN PUBLICATION

Title: Love lives here : a story of thriving in a transgender family / Amanda Jetté Knox.
Names: Jetté Knox, Amanda, author.
Identifiers: Canadiana (print) 20190043806 | Canadiana (ebook) 20190043849 |
ISBN 9780735235175 (softcover) | ISBN 9780735235182 (PDF)
Subjects: LCSH: Jetté Knox, Amanda | LCSH: Jetté Knox, Amanda—Marriage | LCSH:
Parents of transgender children—Canada—Biography. | LCSH: Human rights
workers—Canada—Biography. | LCSH: Sexual minorities' families—Canada. | LCSH:
Transgender people—Family relationships—Canada.
Classification: LCC HQ77.95.C3 J48 2019 | DDC 306.85086/70971—dc23

Cover and interior design by Leah Springate
Cover images: (front) Sarah Driscoll / Unsplash;
(flaps) KanokpolTokumhnerd/Shutterstock.com

Printed and bound in Canada

10 9 8 7 6 5 4 3 2 1

Penguin
Random House
VIKING CANADA

To my family,
who love fiercely
and can patch up a foundation
like nobody's business.

IT'S NOON AND I'M SITTING in a busy coffee shop, a decaf Americano and something called a protein box beside me: eggs and cheese and soft, depressing-looking grapes I won't eat. I'm trying to write the introduction to my family's journey. I've hit backspace more times than I can count, and now I'm taking a moment between attempts to press down on one of the squishy grapes.

Who eats these? Who lives this?

Oh, right. I do. Live it, I mean. Not eat the grapes.

"What do you do for a living?" people often ask when they meet me. It's an easy question. I wish I had an easy answer.

"It's complicated," I want to say, like a Facebook relationship status. And by "complicated," I mean "How do I even begin to tell you that my entire career is founded on an email from an eleven-year-old?"

Somehow, the words "writer and speaker" don't quite cut it—although that's what I generally reply. But my work is deeper than that, because it's fuelled by unconditional love for the people in my life who needed support. First one, then another, and now many.

Love is why I do the work I do. Love is why this book exists. Love for myself, love for my family, love for a whole community of people who don't get enough of it. Can I say I do love for a living, or will people give me a look more withering than the one I've been giving these grapes?

—

Before you read this story, there are some things you should know. Everything in this book is written to the best of my recollection and the recollections of those around me. Memory is an imperfect tool, but the sentiment behind the events described is true. I tried not to embellish, and to recreate conversations as closely as I could. Some names have been changed or left out to protect privacy; I didn't want to throw anyone under the bus, even if some people weren't as kind as they could have been. Finally, in order to keep the focus on the heart of this memoir, I've included only those events relating to how we got here. There are plenty of other stories, but I'll save those for another time.

This book involved the continuous support and input of my family members. It's our collective journey, after all, not just mine. These words wouldn't be nearly as powerful or as meaningful without them.

When writing about trans issues, cisgender people like me—those of us comfortable with the gender we were assigned at birth—should strive to make sure we write nothing that can damage an already marginalized community. Discussions surrounding gender are evolving rapidly, as is the language used.

For this book, I consulted several trans people, but if I messed up anywhere, I apologize. I will strive to do better.

While I hope this book will uplift the reader, there are some tough issues covered, including mental illness, suicidal ideation, sexual assault, gender dysphoria, transphobia, homophobia and LGBTQ slurs. If you find yourself struggling through these pages, please reach out to someone you trust. If you feel alone, there are crisis lines (including LGBTQ-specific ones) and other community supports. Please get the help you need. You deserve to shine.

I use the term "LGBTQ" often in this book. I know our community is bigger than lesbian, gay, bisexual, transgender and queer/questioning people. I did this for brevity, and to avoid constantly referring to "the queer community" (a phrase that, while being reclaimed, has also been used as a weapon). But I see you, asexuals, pansexuals, two-spirit people, intersex people and everyone else who doesn't fit into the first five letters. You are not forgotten.

If you like our family's story, please consider supporting visibly trans and non-binary people. Read their books, blogs and articles. Watch their documentaries, movies and videos. Listen to their podcasts, radio shows and interviews. I promise you'll learn a lot, and as a bonus, you'll be supporting a group of historically marginalized folks who are working hard to turn the tide.

And with that, I will find a compost bin for these squishy grapes and see you on the other side of this book. Thanks for reading.

detour

SHE TOLD ME in the car.

Or rather, she *didn't* tell me. Because it's what wasn't said that gave it all away—the space between our words leaving a silence where you could almost hear our hearts break.

It's funny how much we remember about important moments. That night, a warm summer rain was tapping lightly against the car windows and I could smell the air conditioner as it worked overtime to push out the mugginess of early July. I could hear the splash of puddles as we made our way down the road toward our suburban neighbourhood. I remember how a bright-green grocery store sign lit up the car's interior as I turned and asked that one pivotal question, and how our ten-minute ride home ended up taking well over an hour.

Whenever I think about the night my life changed forever, I'm thrust backwards into sensory overload. The sights, the smells, the sounds are forever a part of the memory. It's only one piece of a much larger story, but I recall it as clearly as I do my children's first breaths or my grandmother's last.

I suppose this makes sense, since that night was both the start of a new life and the end of an old one.

By any measure, it had been a terrible date night. Unbelievably so, even for us. And hey, we knew terrible. Back then, I had a mopey, moody partner. This made everything—including date nights—a lot less fun. How do you have a good time when someone is lugging around misery like a millstone? The person I married barely smiled, even at the best of times. But after more than two decades together, I had come to accept this as our reality. Some people are just not the smiley types, you know?

Oh, *you know*. We all know people like this: the ones you can't coax a grin out of no matter how hard you try. For years, I figured that if I led by example—if I just smiled more, modelled joy or exuded gratitude—the moodiness would disappear. The cloud would lift.

After trying those techniques for so long, and failing spectacularly to get the result I was hoping for, I probably should have known better. Sadly, I'm a killer optimist. I always see a way to let the light in. I'm Charlie Brown running for the football Lucy is holding for me with a mischievous glint in her eye. Damn it, I was going to get the person I'd married to love life, even if it took another two decades. Just watch me.

That's why I'd suggested we go for coffee and cinnamon buns. What kind of person can eat a cinnamon bun without cracking a smile? I was sure I had a foolproof plan as we made our way to Quitters, a quaint hipster establishment owned by the famed musician Kathleen Edwards. In 2014, she had purposefully stepped away from the spotlight to return to Ottawa and open a coffee shop. Her decision garnered much local attention. Who walks away from a career full of accolades to make espressos in the suburbs? People like Kathleen, that's who. Those who seem able to shift from one life to another with much grace and little fear. In hindsight, it seems only fitting that a place that symbolizes so much change would serve as the backdrop to our own seismic shift.

That night, we sat along the back wall in mismatched chairs, a candle dancing on the table between us. I was probably smiling too much and drinking my coffee too fast, which I always do when I'm nervous and fidgety. I know for certain I was asking what was wrong. Because that's what you do on a date night, right? One of you mopes, and the other tries to prod out the cause. They make movies about people like us and release them on Valentine's Day.

"I wish you would just tell me what's going on with you," I said. We sang this little song on a regular basis; we both knew the words.

The person I loved stared out the window. It was nearly dark out; the dim candlelight between us was casting shadows on both our faces. Neither of us was smiling now.

"It's nothing. It's not important." This was the reply that always followed my prodding.

"It *is* important, and I don't buy that it's nothing," I countered, just as I always did. "If it were nothing, you wouldn't be this unhappy all the time."

Unhappy. So unhappy. I was tired of it. Twenty-two years later, it was time to figure out what the hell was going on.

After years spent emotionally propping up our family—like Atlas with an impressive muffin top—I had reached my limit. All that emotional lifting was exhausting and left little room for compassion. Dealing with a spouse in an Eeyore-like state—anger or melancholy oozing out of every pore—and feeling like I had to crank up my own happiness to shield the kids from it all, my magical well of giving a damn had run dry. And there, at the bottom, sat the bitter little troll I'd become.

Because once I had used up all my overcompensating smiles and excessive happiness, once I had tried to make things better yet again, I would land with a thunk on the cold, hard floor of failure. With that, my patience would unravel and the troll would start shouting angrily from the bottom of the well.

"We have a great life!" I often said when I'd reached my breaking point, my voice filled with frustration. "Three amazing kids, a nice home and full bellies. What more could you ask for? Some people would kill for this life! I just don't get you." It was a script I'd memorized.

But not this time. For some reason, I went rogue. For some reason, on this night—in this place of coffee and big changes—I held it together. Somewhere deep down, I must have had a special reserve of patience for this occasion—vintage, stored in fancy bottles with dust on them. I pulled some of that patience out of the cellar and stayed surprisingly calm.

That was a good thing. Because as it turns out, it's hard to open up to someone if that someone is frustrated. This is especially true if you are holding back on sharing a life-altering secret out of fear of your entire world falling apart.

I'm glad I drew from my reserve that night. By not getting angry, I changed the pattern. I likely saved us another twenty-two years of dysfunctional dancing. Unfortunately, I took what normally would have been a bad evening and turned it into a truly terrifying one. Because what would be revealed in the car on the ride home would shatter the life I thought we had. In just a few minutes, I would be staring at the rubble beneath my feet and wondering what the hell I had just done.

But hey, at least I had good intentions.

foundations

TO UNDERSTAND THAT MOMENT in the car, it's important to understand the people in the car—where we came from and how we got there. It's important to know that this was by no means the first time rubble lay at our feet.

Like any great story, mine began at the mall. My mom met my biological father at Bayshore, a large shopping centre in the west end of Ottawa. A university student, my mom worked part time at a now-defunct clothing retailer, and my father was an assistant manager at a children's shoe store. They fell hard for each other. My mom, Elizabeth, was a strikingly beautiful nineteen-year-old of British and Irish heritage, long blonde hair framing a fresh face. My father was Ojibwa, with gorgeous dark wavy hair, a great smile and an angular nose I would inherit and resent throughout my teen years.

My mom found out about me five months into the pregnancy. She went to the doctor, convinced she had an ulcer, and was told that instead of a hole, she had a baby in her stomach. Surprise!

My impending arrival came as a shock to everyone, but especially to Liz and her boyfriend.

Family members insisted they get married and "do things right." So they did. There are pictures of them at their wedding shower, holding up stereotypically seventies-themed china and looking happy. This was the dream for the budding couple, right? A marriage, a family and a grown-up life? It just came a little sooner than expected. A little less time at the mall holding hands and a little more pushing a baby stroller.

My mom has said it was impossible not to fall in love with my father. He was smart, charming and incredibly funny. "Everybody loved him," she's told me many times. Other family members have said similar things. He was the life of any party, a natural comic filled with charisma. He could make the whole room think or laugh, or both.

I wouldn't know. He left when I was a few months old, seemingly disconnected from his young bride and his blonde, curly-haired baby girl. I don't remember a thing about him, but when I look at photos, I have to admit I'm a perfect mix of both my biological parents. I have her colouring and smile, and his high cheekbones, thick hair and, yes, nose. I've made peace with the nose, but I'm still working on making peace with his absence.

I like to think we all have a foundation upon which we build our lives. The more fortunate among us have a solid foundation from the get-go—one constructed from love, trust, stability and support. Some of us are not so lucky, and the events we experience early on leave cracks in our foundation that make for rickety lives. The first crack in my foundation was my father's departure. It has shaped my life in ways I'm still trying to understand.

My mom ended up falling in love again, this time with a man who saw us as a package deal. Charlie, my dad—he has certainly earned the title—has been in my life since he met my mom at a mutual friend's music performance when I was eighteen months old. I never felt like I wasn't his child, even when he and my mom went on to have more children of their own. He treated me no differently from my siblings, which is a testament to his commitment to me. He was the first person to show me that love makes a family—full stop. It needn't be more complicated than that.

Still, little me found out at a young age that my biological father had left, and this created a gaping hole in my foundation for the pain to pour in. Children often internalize the actions of others, and I was no exception. In my young mind, he had left because he didn't love me, and he didn't love me because somehow I was unlovable. The feeling was as deeply ingrained in me as my DNA. Now that I'm older, I know there are many factors that contributed to him not being a part of my life—factors that had nothing to do with me. But for years, I carried the shame of abandonment, and shame is not a good life-building material. It's ugly and porous.

This, in part, is why I worked so hard to get people to like me. It's why I would try to be the funniest, sunniest girl everywhere I went. Like the father I never knew, I would turn on the charm and people would react in positive ways. "Isn't Amanda the greatest kid?" I would hear my parents' friends say. "You must be so proud of her."

I fed off that validation. It filled me up and made me smile. Little Amanda was sunny, funny and charming. She knew it because people told her so. If people liked her, maybe that meant her biological dad was wrong. Maybe she really *was* lovable.

Just not at school. She was anything but lovable there.

—

Three hours away and three years before I was born, there came into the world a baby who was going to face an internal struggle most of us can't begin to imagine.

When that child was born, the doctors looked between the legs and declared it a boy. This is how things were done. Genitals = gender. Society wasn't having meaningful conversations about gender identity—that was stisll decades away. But that little child, who everyone assumed was a boy, knew from an early age that "boy" didn't fit.

This child was given a traditionally masculine name, but I won't be sharing that here. In the transgender community, using someone's old name is often referred to as "deadnaming." It shouldn't be done without permission because it can bring up a great deal of pain and put the person at risk. Yet despite the masculine name she was given and the gender marker stamped on her birth certificate, this child was always *she*. She was always *she*, even if the world perceived her as *he* and told her she belonged in that box, that category, that life.

But it should be noted that she was never a boy.

Peterborough, Ontario, served as the backdrop of her formative years. A mostly blue-collar, hockey-loving, factory-filled Canadian town of about sixty thousand people, it was not the place to declare a gender other than the one you were assigned at birth. But in all fairness, there wasn't a place anywhere in the world at that time for a kid to make such a declaration. To do so would mean ridicule and perhaps even violence. To do so would mean conversion therapy—the standard medical treatment of the time, used to attempt to force that child into identifying as a boy.

And so, this child hid and pretended to be a boy, answering to that masculine name and playing the role of *he* and *him*.

She grew up shy and introverted, with few friends. Her biological mother, like my biological father, didn't stick around. After divorce and a period of messy visitations, the mother packed up, left town and was never seen again. The girl from Peterborough and her younger brother were left in the care of a loving single father, who went on to marry a kind and compassionate woman who would fill the role of mother.

I often try to picture what it must have been like to be a male-presenting child who knew otherwise but had no one to confide in and no access to this gift of information we call the internet. I try to picture it, and I sometimes cry about it. I might not have had the easiest time in my formative years, but I never felt wrong in the body I was born in, or with the gender I was assigned because of it. That's a deeper level of pain than I can imagine.

—

When I started kindergarten, I was one of the youngest in my class because my birthday fell on September 1. Being the class baby didn't score me any points—nor did being one of the only English-speaking kids in a school full of francophones. We lived in Aylmer, Quebec, just across the border from Ottawa. It was the early eighties, and Quebec had spent several years seeking independence from Canada, fed by generations of ugly divide.

We were just on the other side of the October Crisis and other terrorist attacks in the name of sovereignty, and tensions were still high.

In an attempt to ensure that Quebec retained its language and proud culture, the government introduced and strictly enforced Bill 101, the Charter of the French Language. Part of that charter deemed that if a child's parents hadn't been instructed predominantly in English when they were young, that child must attend a francophone school. And so, five-year-old me—a child who spoke very little French and was only nominally Catholic—was put into a French-Catholic school a few blocks from our home.

It's a challenge to turn on the charm in a language you don't understand, and I was left awkwardly trying to comprehend what everyone was saying. There was no way to show the other kids that I was sunny and funny. There would be no external validation to feed my sense of belonging. I had entered new and uncomfortable territory.

Typically, little cliques formed in the class and spilled into the schoolyard. I was desperately trying to figure out where I fit in when I found a small cluster of English kids who looked just as terrified as I was. We played together out of necessity. Even the francophone children who didn't ignore us weren't exactly kind to us. Despite the language barrier, we could see we were disliked. Getting yelled at or shoved was a solid indicator. Being called a *"maudite Anglo"*—a damn Anglo—was another. Looking back, I'm guessing some of these kids were going home to families determined to see Quebec become its own country, and they were probably overhearing conversations at the dinner table about how English-speaking Canada was to blame for many of their problems. They would then bring this sentiment to school with them, and we *maudites Anglos* felt it.

While some of the Anglo kids found their way into other circles over the next few months as they picked up more French, the rest of us never really became a part of the social fabric, no matter how hard we tried. I was one of them. To this day, my mom says I was simply "too nice," and that it's often the nicest people who become the biggest targets. It's true that I tried hard to be kind to those who were cruel, and never fought back when I was mocked or pushed around. Add in the language barriers, and it created a volatile mix of failed people-pleasing and insecurity.

This exclusion caused another crack in my foundation—another reminder that I was less sunny, less funny and less lovable than I thought.

—

In Peterborough, the girl who wasn't seen as one made her way to the library.

She was looking for answers to questions she had kept secret for a very long time. If she was a girl in the way she thought and felt, why didn't she look like one? Why did she have the body she had—the one she was told belonged to a boy? Why wasn't she developing the way the other girls her age were, with a hint of hips and breasts and a softness to her face? Why, instead, was her body changing in ways that felt completely alien? These thoughts were weighing heavily on her mind. But she didn't have anyone to talk to about them. Who would understand? So she turned to whatever reading materials she could dig up.

As she steered her way toward the children's section in the brown brick building on Aylmer Street, her long, graceful fingers ran across book spines and flipped through pages. After an exhaustive but unproductive search, she moved into adult non-fiction, poring over books on anatomy and puberty, looking for a medical explanation of what was happening inside her. But she found nothing about experiences like hers—only chapters full of *shoulds*.

Females in this age group *should* look like this.

They *should* see these changes.

They *should* feel this way.

The books told her she should, but she didn't and she couldn't, no matter how hard she tried. Her body, filled with an abundance of the wrong hormones, was transforming her into what society defined as a pubescent boy.

The only place she found mention of experiences like hers was inside a couple of psychiatry books. What she was going through was a fetish, these books explained. It was sexual, deviant and a sign of mental illness. There was something terribly wrong with her. Mortified, she pushed these books aside. Was this who she was? Was she sick? Shame wormed its way into every part of her. She could see no way out, no way to right this wrong. Research had failed her, and she found herself feeling more alone than ever.

Utterly defeated and on the verge of tears, she grabbed her bike and pedalled down the street as fast as she could, hoping to outrun the girl inside of her.

—

I did have one good playground friend in my elementary school years. Jasmine and I spent recesses trading stickers, playing marbles and talking about all the things we were going to do together in high school and beyond. She didn't mind how much I loved books and overlooked my awkward Anne of Green Gables phase (braids and all!). I lived in my head much of the time, and she indulged me in my endless imaginary play.

In the years Jasmine and I weren't in the same class—by far the worst years for me—I would stand outside at recess and wait for her to join me. Groups of kids would run by, name-calling, but they didn't bother me nearly as much as the two girls who liked to approach me directly. They would find wherever I was waiting, a lone target to prey on.

"What are you doing?" the more forceful one would ask.

"Waiting for my friend," I'd reply in my best French, trying not to make eye contact. "She'll be here any minute."

"What's that?" the sidekick would ask, looking at whatever I had in my hands.

Damn it. I knew this dance.

My dad liked to buy me things he knew I'd find special. When I fell in love with the movie *E.T. the Extra-Terrestrial*, he bought packs of trading cards to surprise me. He would take me out every Friday so I could pick out a Smurf figurine or some cards of the Garbage Pail Kids, a gross parody of Cabbage Patch Kids that was all the rage for a while. I doubt my dad understood my love of them, but he did love seeing me smile when we went to the dépanneur to get them.

"Nice card," one of the girls would say. "I don't have that one yet. Can I see it?"

"No, I don't think so," I'd reply, a part of me hoping it was merely a polite request.

Sometimes they would persuade me with verbal threats, and sometimes one of them would simply hold me while the other wrenched the card or toy out of my hand. I would kick myself for bringing something I cherished to school and go home that day not only ashamed but also guilt-ridden because I'd lost something my dad gave me. I had been so careless with a manifestation of his love, and I worried that he would find out and be hurt. Or even worse, that he would be angry and not want to love me anymore. Just like the man who was supposed to but didn't.

I never fought back against the kids who hurt me. I didn't retaliate against the ones who threw me in a snowbank at every opportunity, holding me face down while I gasped for air. When a girl who had taunted me for months hit me in the face with her metal lunch box one day, bruising my cheek and giving me a black eye, I didn't hit her back. I don't know if it's because part of me believed I deserved it, or if I was simply too scared to stand up against the aggressors. Maybe it was a bit of both. Each time I was bullied in any fashion, I would turn the anger inward. I would berate myself for bringing that special thing to school. I would shame myself for being a target. I would blame myself for not being enough. I would internalize their words, stashing them in a corner of my brain to take out later and replay over and over.

You are worthless. You are meaningless. You are different. You are not enough.

Never enough.

Jasmine's friendship made school bearable. At times, she was my only reason to get up and face another day. But by grade four, she had come to realize that our friendship might be more of a liability to her than an asset.

"You know," she said aloud to me one sunny day, as we stood by a fence overlooking an open field of tall grass, "maybe if I stopped hanging around with you, I could make more friends."

She didn't say it maliciously. She was thinking aloud, as kids often do when they come to a realization. It was honest and painful to hear.

Also, she was probably right.

Over the years, groups of girls had swooped in to try to collect Jasmine, to bring her into their circle. And why not? She was smart, pretty and had plenty of personality. She likely would have been at the top of the social ladder if her mother hadn't worked for the school board. Some kids were willing to overlook that, but they wouldn't overlook me. And since we were a package deal, those offers to join their fun would always fizzle out quickly. Then it would be just the two of us again.

That day, when Jasmine expressed her desire to branch out, my heart sank and I had to focus extra hard on the tall grass swaying in the breeze to stop myself from crying. I didn't look at her when I replied.

"Yeah, maybe. I guess," I said, flustered. "But I thought we were friends."

The bell rang, and I was able to spare myself her reply. That was enough honesty for one recess.

I felt sick for the rest of the afternoon. I was in panic mode, desperately trying to come up with a way to keep my only friend. The crack in my foundation grew wider, deeper and more painful. Someone else I loved was going to leave because I wasn't *enough*, and there wasn't a damn thing I could do about it.

Or maybe there was. An idea was forming.

———

Two years earlier, when I was seven, my parents had sat me down to tell me about my biological father. I was getting older and starting to ask questions about why my last name was different from theirs.

I remember sitting on the kitchen stool, listening to my parents try to explain the unexplainable. My swinging legs stopped dead as my father said, "I'm not the dad who was with you the day you were born—that was another man. Yes, he knows about you. No, he isn't around. No, we don't know why. No, we don't know where he is. We wish we had those answers, sweetie. But I love you and I am your dad."

My head swam with this new information. The man I thought was my father—the man who had been in my life for as long as I could remember—was telling me he only took on the position after someone else resigned.

Hats off to my parents. They tried very hard to persuade me that my biological father's departure had nothing to do with me. They reminded me how loved I was and how special I was, and they explained that grown-ups sometimes make decisions that are hard to understand. They said that I was still their beautiful girl, and that Charlie would always be my dad. Dads, after all, are the men who take on the role.

I wish I could have believed them.

That first crack in my foundation is still the biggest. To this day, abandonment hurts me like little else can. The fear of being left behind began in that moment, on that stool in the kitchen. Because if he could leave, anyone could.

My parents could.

Jasmine could.

Which is probably why, when I heard Jasmine's musings two years later, I came home from school with my heart pounding and my pulse racing. I ran for my art supplies. I spent an inordinate amount of time crafting her a card filled with pictures and sentiments about how special she was to me. It was colourful and happy. I taped whatever coins I could find to the inside and wrote the words "Please still be my friend" beneath them.

The next morning, I presented her with the card and anxiously awaited her response. I needed her not to leave me all alone in that miserable schoolyard. She mulled it over for most of the day, and ultimately decided we could stay friends. At least in the short term. But she didn't rule out setting off on her own in the future.

That was the first of a handful of times I made a card like that and held it out for Jasmine to read, my stomach in knots. Yes, you read that right: I literally paid someone to be my friend. I was willing to do anything at all to keep the pain away, including reducing myself to a few coins and the promise to try to be a better friend to someone who, frankly, didn't deserve that friendship.

THREE

self-destruction

THREE HOURS AWAY, the girl in Peterborough was struggling to get through school. She was smart, studious and talented. She was driven, capable and organized. Thanks to her naturally inquisitive mind, she was a teacher's dream, learning with ease and excelling at anything she took an interest in. There was just one problem: she didn't excel at playing the role of a guy. She looked like one—with her short black hair and enviable height— but an innate femininity lived inside her and emanated outward, no matter how hard she tried to hide it. She had been teased for this for as long as she could remember.

"You're a fag!" the boys would yell, hitting the girl they thought was a boy. They followed her around, doing their best to make her life miserable. They stole her bike and kicked her as she lay on the ground, trying not to cry. Every day was a nightmare.

The confused and hurting girl who could find no others like her—no examples of girls who had to pretend to be boys—was hurting deeply. She had no answers to why she felt as she did, and no safe person to confide in. She thought about telling her parents who she really was, but how could she even begin that conversation? And what could they do to help her, even if they believed her?

Things got so bad that she had to switch high schools. The school board had been sending her to class in a taxi every day because she was harassed on the bus. At her new school, she learned to keep her head down and focus on her studies. As she grew older, she became more adept at hiding who she was. The girl worked harder at playing the role of *he* and *him*. She studied masculinity and tried her best to model it. But this inauthenticity came at a cost. The softness within her grew hard; the sweetness grew sour. Eventually, hurt and fear boiled down into anger and festered inside her. She was sullen one moment, full of rage the next. Her heart was at war with her brain.

Her parents didn't know what to do to help this girl they thought of as the elder of two sons. Her anger was bordering on dangerous, her grades were slipping and her life was falling apart. They had her speak with doctors and psychologists, but no one could get to the root of the problem because she dared not say what it was.

By sixteen, she was living on the streets of Toronto, charging headlong into a self-destructive spiral.

———

Meanwhile, a perfect storm was brewing in my own life.

I'd started grade seven at a large francophone secondary school. There were no middle schools in the French system at the time—no hormonal thirteen- and fourteen-year-olds smushed together into our own building until we maxed out our growth spurts. Nope, we were playing in the big leagues, walking among giants, from the very first pimple.

Thankfully, I fell into a small but welcoming group of girls that included my childhood friend, Emmy. Her grandparents lived in my neighbourhood. We didn't attend the same elementary school, but we spent our weekends and summers together. Emmy introduced me to her friends, and because they had no idea about my social-pariah past, I hoped this would be my fresh start. Despite my best efforts to reinvent myself in this new space, however, my reputation as an awkward social pushover soon became known. Melanie and Sylvia, inseparable friends who were definitely not *my* friends—once they had chased me down the road, trying to throw lit matches in my hair while laughing hysterically—were forging connections in our new school, and they introduced me as a target to a whole new group of people.

An older boy pointed at me as I walked down the hall alone one day. "Is that her?" he asked, loudly enough for me to hear him. He was in the school's rock band. He flashed a handsome smile, and his sandy-blond hair flipped over his shoulder as he turned back to Sylvia and Melanie and his other friends. "You're right. She's a total dog. Fugly."

I had learned long before this that engagement was almost always bad. I walked away that time, the next time and the time after that too. I was a good walker-away-er. But as I walked away, the sandy-haired boy and his friends started following me down the hall, calling me Zenji, which was a hybrid of Benji (a well-known movie dog from the seventies) and the word "zits."

Zenji: a dog with zits.

That name spread through the school like acne had spread across my face that year. Puberty had not been kind to me. I grew my bangs out and wore my hair down to shield as much of the pimply redness as possible. I came to hate what I saw in the mirror.

"Hey, Zenji!" kids would say when I arrived at my locker. They would bark at me when I walked into the cafeteria, collapsing in laughter at their own cleverness. My few friends stood by me, but quietly, not wanting to become targets themselves.

"See?" I told myself while I was getting ready one morning. "It was just a matter of time before everyone figured it out." Everything I had feared about high school was rearing its unwelcome head: the loneliness, isolation and mockery. It was consuming me. The Zenji "joke" went on for months, and things soon got worse.

I started drinking—just a little at first, but the habit grew quickly. We had a liquor cabinet at home that nobody touched, its dusty bottles sitting on the shelf for years. No one noticed when the contents began to disappear. I would stash a mickey in my locker at school and take swigs between classes. It was just enough to take the edge off.

But nights alone in my room were the hardest. I watched endless MuchMusic videos and wrote songs with the five or six chords I knew on guitar. I felt empty and hopeless.

My last day at my first high school ended up being one of the hardest of my life. There are pieces of that day I can't remember—a common occurrence with traumatic events. But here's what I do recall: I was standing outside alone, watching a handful of other people smoke cigarettes or chat with their friends. Before I knew it, a group of students had filed out of the building and gathered around me. They were the guys from the band, some of their fans, and Melanie and Sylvia. They all looked to be waiting for something. I immediately tensed up.

Melanie, I noticed, had a bottle of hairspray. Sylvia was

clutching a box of matches. It took me only a second to understand what they were about to do.

Melanie walked up and started spraying me. It was a repeat of the time they had chased me down the road, laughing and trying to set me on fire. Except this time, they had an audience.

"Want to see Zenji dance? Let's make her dance!"

Even in the open air, I could smell the alcoholic stench of the hairspray on my thick cotton sweater. I turned away.

"Please stop!" I yelled. "Stop it!"

Adrenaline flooded through me. I knew I had to run, but they were quicker. My back went up in flames.

Anyone nearby would have seen me: a screaming girl with flames shooting up her back, throwing herself onto the grass and rolling around to extinguish them. They would have seen me stand up, covered in dry grass and leaves, my pants stained and sweater charred. They would have seen me looking around at the sea of shocked faces (and a few amused ones) and bursting into tears.

One girl emailed me a few years ago to say she still remembers that awful moment and regrets not stepping in to stop it. To be fair, I don't think anyone could have. The bullying had been building for years. Had this not been the climax, it would have been something else.

I don't remember much of the rest of the day, except that my parents were notified and arrived at the school understandably upset. A meeting took place with the principal, then we packed up my things and I never attended that school again. It was no longer safe.

Most of the damage done by bullying is internal. The lasting harm comes not from what the bully says or does at the time, but from how often the victims replay the events in their minds and chastise themselves for not responding differently. It's how what is said to us festers and morphs into what we say to ourselves. Bullying is like a snakebite: the initial attack stings, but it's the after-effects that can kill you.

My foundation had new cracks in it. I knew it, but I didn't know to fix them, and I didn't try. The damage had been done; the basement was flooding, and I was sitting in it, waiting to drown—*hoping* to, in fact. Those giving me grief could have walked off the job sooner. No one needed to be cruel to me any longer; I was doing a fine job on my own.

Over the next few months, I continued to self-destruct. Severe anxiety and depression took hold. My drinking escalated, and I found myself unable to stop, despite my best efforts. I told my parents through sobs that I needed help. My mom pulled in every resource she could find, but in 1991, there weren't many options for a fourteen-year-old. Most facilities didn't know how to deal with someone my age who was abusing substances. If I'd been even a year or two older, they might have had a place for me.

Finally, after I wound up drunk and high with strange adults on more than one occasion and went missing for days at a time, a treatment facility took my parents' cries for help seriously. On June 13, 1991, my dad drove me to Alwood, a six-month live-in treatment program for teens and young adults just outside of Ottawa. We both cried as he drove away.

Alwood offered group sessions, individual counselling, art and music therapy, meditation and nature walks. It was situated in a beautiful old brick farmhouse surrounded by fields and forest. The staff and other residents were friendly and upbeat. They ate together, laughed together, sang songs together and supported one another. All I had to do over the next six months was buy in like everyone else had, do what was asked of me and focus on learning new life skills.

I hated it.

I was full of attitude, sullen and angry for the first half of my stay. I didn't know how to be Amanda anymore. Spending all day, every day, patching up your foundation is heavy work. Growth is never a straight line. I clashed with staff members, played victim in nearly every situation and got called out more times than I can count. I nearly got kicked out twice, and I was told maybe I was too immature to handle the program. I could have left. Because it had a lengthy waiting list of teens and young adults desperate for help, Alwood insisted its residents be willing participants in their recovery. "Don't take up space someone else would gratefully use," one social worker told me. "We want you to stay, but what matters is that *you* want to."

People came and went. Some stayed a few days, some a few weeks. A handful graduated after the full six months, and a few of them visited to provide hopeful updates on their lives since then. Once out in the world again, some relapsed and found their way back. It was a home in constant transition. The bed beside mine would be in use for a time, then lie vacant until someone else came to fill it.

One day, a staff member pulled me into the office.

"We have a young woman coming in today who's addicted to heroin," she explained. "She was supposed to go to a detox centre first to get through the worst of it. But there was a mix-up, so she's going to do a medically supervised detox here."

Within hours, a woman nearly a decade older than me became my roommate. For the next three days, I watched her suffer through the agony of the powerful drug leaving her body. She would scream for someone to help her with the pain, sweating and clenching her stomach. I would wake up in the middle of the night to her moans and sit by her bed until a staff member arrived. What she was going through was so much worse than anything I had ever experienced in my life. And as she got better, she began to share her story with me. The earlier parts sounded a lot like mine.

I realized that I not only wanted to be there but *needed* to be if I was going to make it to adulthood. I dug in and worked harder.

In December 1991, to the surprise of everyone, I became the youngest person at that time to graduate from the program. I was six months sober and as ready as I could be to rejoin the world. I emerged a more confident and assertive fifteen-year-old, with a smile on my face and plans for my future. I had my life back. I was starting to figure out who I was, and she wasn't so bad.

I returned to Aylmer and started bumping into some of the people who used to bully me. But one fundamental thing had changed: my attitude. I was completely unwilling to be pushed around. There were rumours about where I had been—some people thought I had gone to juvie for petty crimes or had almost died of an overdose. I laughed them off. The kids who used to hurl insults at me quickly learned it was futile to continue. Instead of giving them the reaction they were looking for, I would just smile, shrug and keep walking. The spell had been broken.

Today we know that some young people who develop a dependency on substances when struggling with acute mental illness can go on to have a healthy relationship with alcohol once the primary issue has been dealt with. But if you were a teen abusing alcohol in 1991, the standard treatment was lifelong sobriety. It was just as well. Sobriety became a tool I used for twenty-five years to shape my life in healthy ways. After that solid chunk of time, and following several conversations with the right professionals, I tried drinking socially again.

If I'm an alcoholic, I'm doing a really bad job at relapsing. I barely touch the stuff. But I wouldn't take back the years I spent sober, or what it took to get me there. The lessons I learned are worth more than all the Pinot Grigio I missed out on. And because of the path those lessons put me on, I found myself across the table from the one person who would change everything. What we had both experienced in childhood was simply preparing us for a future that would require an abundance of resiliency. Our shaky foundations were about to come together to build something new.

gravitation

I MET THE LOVE of my life on May 1, 1993. I was sixteen and had been living on my own for the previous few months. My experiences had changed me. I no longer felt like a child, but I was still leading a child's life. My relationship with my parents had been strained over the past couple of years, and time away hadn't repaired it. We argued far too much, and a lot of my negative behaviours were coming back. It just wasn't working. I left two months after my sixteenth birthday, with fifteen dollars in my pocket, half a pack of smokes and a determined look on my face.

For six months, I slept on couches, in someone's spare bedroom, at the downtown YMCA-YWCA, in a couple of rooming houses that would take someone my age and even in an apartment stairwell. It was a relatively short but critical part of my life. I was just beginning to find my footing, and the last thing I was looking for was a relationship.

Even at that young age, my romantic track record was already sketchy. When I was fourteen, my virginity had been taken by force by a nineteen-year-old drug dealer on an old basement couch on New Year's Eve. The few relationships I'd had since then crossed boundaries in other ways, from infidelity to verbal abuse. I was done with boys. No more. I wasn't sure what the appeal was, anyway.

I briefly thought about dating girls—particularly the one who told me she had a crush on me. The thought was short-lived. I didn't want to stand out any more than I had for most of my life. Always an outcast, I now just wanted to blend in, to be part of the fabric of society. The easiest way to do that was to find the right guy. But not yet. First, I had some fundamentals to figure out: finding a stable place to live, getting a job, going to school and making sure I had enough to eat. These were my daily priorities. I had no room in my life for dating.

But I did like parties. There was room in my life for those.

A few weeks earlier, I had moved into a nice halfway house on Gloucester Street in downtown Ottawa. The spacious three-storey red-brick home was a breath of fresh air. It was clean and quiet. The organization that ran it provided rooms to adults in recovery or living with mental health issues. At sixteen, I wasn't an adult, but I was nearly two years sober and had dealt with my fair share of mental illness. Because of this, they made an exception for me. It meant a warm home, three meals a day, my own room on the third floor with a window overlooking the neighbouring church and access to counselling services. I was, and remain, deeply grateful that they took a chance on me.

It was there I met Sandra, a young Indigenous woman full of humour and enthusiasm. One night, Sandra and her boyfriend, Ben, were going to a friend's birthday party, and I scored a last-minute invitation. I threw on a black off-the-shoulder sweater and made sure my curls had extra bounce. Sandra and Ben were a bit older than me, and I wanted to make a good impression on their friends.

The party was in a nondescript apartment building in the city's east end. We made our way to a large event room in the basement. It was dark, save for the DJ lights bouncing off balloons and streamers affixed to the ceiling tiles. The music was a mix of eighties new wave and early nineties rock. I grabbed a Coke and sat down with a group of Sandra and Ben's friends. It was nice to get out and meet people.

After about an hour, I excused myself and went down the hall to find the bathroom and reapply my nineties-era Jennie Garth dark lipstick. When I came back into the room, I saw a very good-looking person sitting at the table.

"This is Ben's roommate," Sandra said.

I smiled and held out my hand.

—

The girl from Peterborough had moved to Ottawa to go to school. At twenty, she presented herself to the world as a young, attractive man. This is not what she wanted, not who she knew herself to be, but life had continued to show her that there were no other avenues to pursue. This was how she had to live. This was what she had to pretend to be.

She was taking a computer science program at Algonquin College while staying in a house with Ben and some other students. A few months earlier, away from her small town and the judgment she would certainly have faced there, she had taken a bold step forward. With a female friend's permission, she had gone through her wardrobe and borrowed some of her clothes.

She wanted to see how they looked, how they felt. She stared into the mirror and, for the first time, saw a glimmer of her true self staring back. She smiled shyly at her reflection.

The girl worked up the courage to wear those clothes around the house and hoped she would be well received by the people she called friends. In this large city, in this place away from everyone she had grown up with, where she finally felt a sense of safety, it was her moment to tell everyone who she really was. She could build a new life.

She took a deep breath and made her way downstairs.

At first, they met her with laughter. They thought she was being funny. A dude dressing up as a lady to make his buddies double over. When they realized that she wasn't joking—that she was dead serious—their amusement turned to concern and anger.

"You can't do this here," they told her.

"But this is who I am," she explained. "It's who I've always been."

"No way," they replied, a mix of pity and disgust on their faces. "You need help. Get some. If you start wearing dresses, you can't live here anymore, okay? You'll have to leave."

It had taken nineteen years to work up the courage to dip a toe into the waters of authenticity. It took just minutes to be shut down. Heartbroken and embarrassed, she went back to her room, took off the dress through hot tears and made a solemn decision: she would never utter another word of this to anyone again. No matter the cost, she was going to live as a man.

—

Ben's roommate was a babe—a serious, stone-cold babe. Leather jacket. Sexy hair. Full lips. Guys really didn't do it for me, but this felt different. I wasn't able to put it in these words at the time, but there was a distinct softness, a gentleness that was positively magnetic.

We quickly got lost in conversation. I sat, transfixed, across the table from Ben's roommate, who loved new wave music and vegetarian meals, and who seemed as enamoured with me as I could have hoped. A guy unlike any guy I had ever met. A guy who wasn't a guy at all, but was trying so hard to be.

One month later, we signed a lease and moved into an apartment together. Me and the person I knew as my boyfriend. We lived above some drug dealers and a massive Rottweiler that often made it impossible for us to enter our upstairs flat from the front door in our shared hallway. Instead, we would climb up the rickety back steps, icy in the Ottawa winter, and laugh about our luck. We were starving students—truly hungry a lot of the time—subsisting on noodles made in hand-me-down pots and pans from my parents. I was finishing high school and would proudly tell anyone who listened that my boyfriend was taking computer science in college. We had a rescued kitten that would curl up between us while we watched *The X-Files* on Sunday nights. We always spent our last pennies of the month at a trendy little coffee shop in the ByWard Market. We would read, sketch, play chess and hang out with our artsy, geeky friends. We were poor, but it was a magical time.

Had we moved too fast? I had leapt with both feet into the relationship and spent hours justifying the decision to my parents and close friends. When I announced I was leaving the halfway house, the director of the program, who barely knew me, had yelled at me in her cubicle in front of other staff members.

"What do you mean you're moving in with him?"

"I'm in love," I said, my face hot with embarrassment.

"You're in love?" she replied, astounded. "You don't even know what love is!"

"I know I love him. That's what matters."

"No, you don't. You're sixteen. When I was sixteen, I had no clue what love was. Neither do you."

I left her office barely managing to hold in the angry tears and determined to prove her wrong.

And I *would* prove her wrong, but it wouldn't exactly be a smooth ride.

The drug-dealing neighbours got worse over time, so we moved to the far west end of the city—as far away as two poor kids with no car could manage. Kanata was the end of the line for buses and student budgets. It was the whitest and wealthiest place I had ever lived. Our street of rental row houses stood out among the large suburban homes with their manicured lots.

Where we used to blend in, we now stood out. Cashing my welfare cheque, which was helping me pay the bills while I went to high school, was never a pleasant experience. I always felt that all eyes were on me—from the other clients to the bank tellers. The shame I felt leaving with my monthly deposit slip would linger for days.

The friends we met in the suburbs lived at home with parents who weren't fond of their children spending time with two young people who lived alone. Even though we were sober and going to school, we had no jobs and kept late hours when we weren't in class.

"My mom thinks you're a bad influence," one of our friends told us. "She said if I stop hanging out with you, she'll buy me a new car."

I felt like Zenji all over again in the burbs. And when, nearly three years into our relationship, we found out I was expecting, I became a pregnant nineteen-year-old in a place where pregnant nineteen-year-olds stuck out like a sore thumb. I wondered what my friend's mom would give him not to be seen with me now. Maybe he would get a new house.

My next thought was that we needed to move out of the suburbs.

Aerik was born on November 30, 1996. He was ten pounds and six ounces of adorableness. The moment I held him was transformational in a way no one could have explained to me until I experienced it. Motherhood packs a mighty punch.

"Don't mess this up," a voice inside me said as I gazed upon my child for the first time. I was twenty years old. Six years earlier, I had been in a rehab centre, fighting my way through depression and substance abuse. Life had been in a state of flux ever since. I had yet to finish high school and was working far too slowly on correspondence courses. We were living on one modest income, well below the poverty line, and I had no clue what I wanted to do with my life. Now we had a baby, and the reality of the situation was unfolding before me.

Don't mess this up, Amanda. You can't mess this up.

integration

"I DON'T UNDERSTAND these people!" I yelled over the TV, startling baby Aerik, who had fallen asleep at the breast. A couple were arguing on a talk show and making a complete spectacle of their relationship. Watching them fight was a guilty pleasure, an escape from the humdrum of new motherhood.

We had moved back downtown shortly before our son was born, into a dark and narrow semi-detached home that was never meant to be split in two. I had already seen three cockroaches in the kitchen. The furnace stopped working right before Christmas, and the landlord made no apologies for it when he got back from Florida a few days later.

Because I'd left school rather than a job to have a baby, I had no maternity-leave pay. We existed on what my partner made working for a small local internet service provider, and it was just above minimum wage. What we could afford downtown was half the size of what we could get in the suburbs. Because the area we were in was a patchwork of diversity, however, we attracted less unwanted attention as young parents.

We were happy. I mean, sort of. We were happier than the couple on the talk show, arguing over who slept with whose best friend first. We were certainly happier than the middle-aged neighbours across the street, who seemed to take rotating shifts moving in and out of their apartment between fights.

Compared to them, we were Brady Bunch bliss.

But we were a muted sort of happy. Or maybe, I sometimes wondered, a muted sort of unhappy? It was hard to tell. We sat in a space between big emotions, in calm but overcast waters. A sea of grey. We didn't fight much, but we didn't laugh much either. We didn't drink coffee together on the porch like we used to, but who had the time? We were three now, not two. We had made a family, and maybe this was how families were. Maybe this was the new grey kind of happy. I looked at my sleeping baby and wondered, not for the first time, if we had perhaps jumped in too far or too soon.

—

The girl from Peterborough, now twenty-three, a lanky six feet with dark hair and thick brows that made her green eyes pop, was trying hard to be a man. In the past three years, she had done all kinds of straight, manly guy things. She had met a girl, settled down, got a job and had a baby. And now she was trying to be that baby's father.

The problem was, she wasn't a dad. Although she looked like one, was told she was one and had seen her name printed on the baby's birth certificate next to the word "father," the role fitted her as badly as the clothes she wore, the name she was called by and the shame she carried for not feeling right in the life she was building.

But she would keep trying. She wasn't one to give up, and she knew she could make this role work if she just kept moving in the right direction. She loved the girl she'd met at that party three years earlier. She loved the baby they'd made together. And she would be what they needed, no matter what.

—

We were married on August 16, 1997. A glance at the wedding photos—none of them professional, since we couldn't afford a photographer—reveals a bride and groom, young, in love and ready to start their lives. Friends and family surround them, and a baby is often glued to one of their hips. In some pictures, they stand outside a small United Church on Island Park Drive. In others, they're dancing to Blue Rodeo's "Lost Together" across the river at the marina in Aylmer, Quebec, while several dozen guests look on.

Grey still surrounded us much of the time, but that day was special. I held my spouse—"my husband!" I would exclaim for weeks, until the newness wore off—close to me as we danced. There was a lot of love between us. There was also a giant wall in the way, big and invisible, but we were able to climb to the top of it that day and connect with passion.

Our son was eight months old when we said our vows. He was terrified of my nineties bride hair and poofy rental dress. He didn't recognize me. But then, I hardly recognized myself. In the span of four years, I had fallen in love, had a surprise pregnancy, become a mother and gotten hitched. From lost soul to somebody's mom, from lonely girl to somebody's wife, in what felt like the blink of an eye. Barely an adult with all the adult responsibilities and a relationship issue I couldn't quite put my finger on.

—

When I was twenty-two, we moved back to my hometown of Aylmer and bought a starter home in a new neighbourhood with no trees and plenty of babies. My spouse had managed to get a job at a large high-tech company, which meant we had defied demographics and were able to climb out of poverty as a young couple with a child. This was the first time our family broke the statistical mould, but it wouldn't be the last.

It was strange bumping into people I had once known, my toddler in tow. Some were old friends, some weren't but were now friendly, and others were people I remembered who didn't remember me at all. One especially awkward encounter happened in the produce section of Loblaws, where I spotted Sylvia. Like me, she was pushing a cart with a child in it.

My breath caught and my chest tightened. This was someone who had made my life miserable, smeared my reputation with new people in a new place and then set me on fire. There is no etiquette guide to handling situations like these.

I took a deep breath and turned my cart in her direction. A decade had gone by; we were adults now, and both mothers living in the same town. It was time to bury the hatchet, right?

"Sylvia?"

She turned and looked at my smiling face. As recognition set in, her own face darkened.

"I'm not sure if you remember me," I said. "I'm Amanda. We went to school together."

"Oh, I remember you," came the reply, disgust oozing out

of it. Her expression and body language screamed hostility. The preschooler in her cart was playing with a bunch of bananas, seemingly unaware of his mother's sudden change in mood.

"Is this your son?" I asked.

"Yep," she replied curtly.

"He's so cute," I said, struggling to lighten the mood. "This is mine. They look to be about the same age."

Commonality is a helpful tool in creating connections—except, apparently, when you're trying to connect with someone who literally set you on fire.

"Yeah. Sure," she said, looking over her shoulder to give me a clear view of how uninterested she was in talking to me. When she met my eyes again, they were as cruel as ever.

"Well," I said, not wanting to prolong the awkwardness any longer, "it was nice seeing you. I hope we run into each other again."

"Uh-huh. Bye." She turned and walked away, her son waving at mine.

I had always wondered what had happened to those girls after I left the school. Were they reprimanded? And if so, how severely? Did the people they were trying to impress turn on them when they realized I could have been seriously hurt or killed? How did that one decision affect the rest of their lives?

I hurt more for her than I did for me when I saw how she handled our surprise reunion. Perhaps her hostility was due to embarrassment over what she had done, or maybe it was just lingering dislike, but a part of her had clearly never left the schoolyard. What must it be like to be locked in time, your raw emotions frozen for years? I had worked through that pain in therapy. I had moved on, but she hadn't.

"And that," I said, looking down at my young son with a smile, "is how you treat people with kindness, even when they don't give it back. Rise above, okay? Always remember that."

—

Imposter syndrome is the inability to internalize your own successes, and it has wrapped its wicked tendrils around my mind for as long as I can remember. Someone with imposter syndrome is always waiting to be exposed as a fake and run out of her life. I have a formal diagnosis of it, which is not something I'm proud of. I can't remember a time when I didn't feel like a giant fraud.

Being a mother did not automatically make me feel like I was part of the sacred circle of motherhood. Holding a mortgage did not make me feel like a grown-up. And nothing made me feel as if I belonged in the life I was leading. After all, we'd had an unexpected pregnancy, followed by a shoestring wedding, and we weren't as fairy-tale happy as I'd thought we would be. Everyone in this new neighbourhood seemed to be educated and gainfully employed, and I didn't even have a high school diploma, let alone much job experience. I was waiting for someone to reveal all that, and to upend my life again.

Our house was nestled between the homes of two couples who were very close. We bought the middle house after it had been vacant for almost a year. When we pulled up with the keys, the neighbours were hanging out in our backyard. I opened the patio doors and said a friendly hello. They looked at me as if I was imposing—on my own property—and slowly dispersed like teenagers who had been caught loitering. For the next few years, they rarely spoke to us.

To early-twenties me, this was a clear sign of what an impos-ter I was. The neighbours didn't want us there, and therefore we didn't belong there. I felt buried by their judgment, and anxiety welled up whenever I went outside. Our yard was the schoolyard all over again, and I avoided it whenever they were in theirs. Meanwhile, I tried to make our life appear ideal to anyone look-ing in. I made sure that we were courteous and quiet, and that we kept up with all those suburban activities, like washing our cars and planting lush annuals in baskets on the front porch. I didn't want us to be "that" family—the one people had reason to talk about. When I saw both male neighbours pointing their fingers at the number of weeds on our lawn, I spent the next couple of days trying to eliminate all the dandelions. When that didn't work, I insisted we tear up the lawn and order new sod. We spent hundreds of dollars making our front yard into the nicest one on the street. Now our yard, at least, was manageable. What was going on inside the house was not. I could fix the lawn, but I couldn't fix my spouse, who was not only unhappy but also unpredictable, with a temper that flared up quickly.

What we all saw, friends and family both, was a miserable man whose misery didn't seem to stem from the circumstances of his life. He was attractive and in his prime. He had a wife who loved him and an adorable child. He was on the rise at work in the high-tech field. He had two cars in the driveway of a brand-new house. Sure, the neighbours weren't great, but it was nothing some sod couldn't smooth over.

Sometimes I thought it was the demands of work. Sometimes I thought it was undiagnosed depression. But most of the time, I thought it was me. I had a spouse who felt stuck in the responsi-bilities of family life. I worried it was just a matter of time before

I became a single mom—another example of what happens when you marry too young. A statistical inevitability.

But don't worry. A baby fixes everything.

—

"Can I have a little brother?" Aerik asked me one day, his winter boots crunching against the snow on the sidewalk.

"Well, you don't exactly get to pick what you get, you know," I laughed. "But yes, we hope we can give you a sibling soon."

"Good. Because I'm the only kid in my school with no brothers or sisters." He threw his mittened hands up in the air, the four-year-old drama meter hitting a 7.5. "The only one!"

His preschool had only about fifteen kids in it, so this wasn't nearly as unusual as it sounded. But I hadn't realized he was noticing the differences between our family and the families around him. I wondered what else he'd noticed. How young we were? How the neighbours barely spoke to us? How hard I worked at trying to make us fit in?

I had recently been diagnosed with polycystic ovary syndrome, or PCOS, which is a hormonal disorder that can cause a host of problems, including infertility. I watched enviously as friends and family members conceived, carried and birthed their newborns with only minor hiccups. Now I knew that Aerik was watching them too. Having grown up in a family of six, I'd always believed the family I made wouldn't be complete until the kids outnumbered the parents.

Some days, motherhood felt like all I had. See the nice breakfast I made Aerik? See the cute outfit he's wearing? Look at that craft we did together and the pictures from our museum trip this week. Look at how happy he is. Motherhood gave me tangible proof that I could do something good—something right—for once. But it didn't look like it would ever happen again. Twice I had confirmed pregnancies, and each time I lost the baby.

One night, in the middle of miscarrying, I looked toward the sky and spoke to no one in particular. I do this only at times when I feel particularly lost—it's a throwback to my Catholic upbringing.

"Look, I'm not asking for the moon here," I said through tears. God, Allah, Gaia, Buddha, Jesus, the Universe—I figured one of them might be around. "I just want a baby. And I know that seems greedy because I already have one. But I promise, if you help make that happen, I will love that child like you've never seen."

I don't know who was listening that night, but whoever it was made sure I kept my part of the deal.

In 2002, after four years of doctors' visits, treatment plans, negative tests and plentiful tears, a stubborn little egg got together with an equally stubborn sperm. That stubborn little cell cluster would grow into our second child and change our family in a much bigger way than we could have imagined. Somewhere up there, Buddha, Allah and Jesus likely high-fived, taking credit for what was going to happen, while Gaia sat quietly with a knowing grin on her face.

The following few months were some of the most anxious of my life. As my belly swelled, I would lie quietly and wait for kicks to let me know there was life inside. Each checkup was a good one, and all the people around me were excited. But I couldn't reach that excitement—not until I was holding a baby in my arms. I finally got that chance on November 13, 2002. After twenty-seven hours of labour and an emergency Caesarean, I heard the doctors say, "It's a healthy boy!" I felt indescribable relief.

Like a lot of parents, I loved my first-born so much that I worried about being able to love another child as fiercely. What if I couldn't do it? But within seconds of hearing the first healthy cry, that worry melted and my heart opened wider.

Just under four years later, my body did another miraculous thing and made baby number three. Weighing in at a positively svelte ten pounds and two ounces, Jackson was the smallest of the siblings. He was also the bookend baby—the one who made the kids outnumber the parents, and thus put an end to our baby-making. Even though it took a full decade, we had the family I had always dreamed of. Meanwhile, the neighbours on both sides had become parents for the first time. Their lawns weren't looking so pristine anymore! I would walk out of the house proudly with my three kids and greet the new moms with an air of expertise. Welcome to the club, kittens. I've been here awhile and I know a few things.

If you had asked me to describe our family back then, I would have proudly told you we were a mom, a dad and three little boys. Perfect in our typicality, with a nice sodded lawn and everything.

Blending in felt so good.

—

After the arrival of our second child, I opened a home daycare. It was a chaotic and messy business, but a great work-from-home option for a parent with young kids. I had also recently discovered blogs and wanted to start one of my own in my so-called spare time. Six months pregnant with my third child and putting in nine work hours of wiping bums and noses (side note: Bums N' Noses would make an excellent name for a cover band), I needed some form of relief. Writing had always been cathartic for me.

I wanted my blog to be edgy and funny: a less-than-perfect

look at motherhood. At the time, a lot of parenting blogs—or "mommy blogs," as they were often called—showcased the best of parenthood: perfect crafts, delicious recipes and clean, happy children. I could relate. Much of my life was spent trying my hardest to look exactly like that. As a young and formally uneducated mom, I overcompensated in everyday life. I *was* that blog, and keeping up the facade was exhausting. No one can be that perfect.

Instead, I wanted my blog to be honest, humorous and relatable—something that reached underneath the surface of motherhood and scratched an itch we all needed scratched. When it came time to create a name for it, though, I paused. What do you call the sage voice of chaos?

And then it came to me.

"The Maven of Mayhem," I said out loud as I typed.

Perfect.

I ended up closing the daycare shortly before Jackson was born, but kept the blog. Wise choice.

—

A few months after becoming a family of five, we moved from our starter home to one a mile down the road, in the same neighbourhood I grew up in and my parents still lived in. It had more square footage and a half-acre yard for the kids to play in. Our 1946 post-war house needed lots of work. But a giant tree with a tire swing and floorboards that creaked when we walked down the halls gave us the charm we were looking for after years of living in a cookie-cutter house. The neighbourhood association had family events, from corn roasts to sleigh rides. The retired neighbours across the street, Len and Claire, welcomed us immediately, and we spent many hours drinking coffee on each other's front steps. I got gardening tips from Claire (the world of perennials was new to me), and Len would bring out popsicles for the kids whenever he saw them outside on a hot day. Most importantly, in a neighbourhood this relaxed, weeds were more than acceptable.

The house, the neighbourhood, our family—all of it screamed "typically average." I loved it.

For years, I had wanted nothing more than to feel like I fit into the life I was leading. I'd wanted to own my existence as a mom, wife and budding writer. I might have called myself the Maven of Mayhem, but I often dreamed of being the Tyrant of Typicality. When your world has been turned upside down a few times—and especially when you suffer from sometimes crippling anxiety—it's not unreasonable to want normal as your main course at the buffet of life.

Here, finally, was my normal. My average family and I lived in the town where I grew up, in the very neighbourhood where everything was familiar. And I could now walk those familiar streets with my head held high because I had done well in life, despite everything I'd gone through.

If your foundation is solid, you can do just about anything. For the first time, mine felt earthquake-proof.

roots

"YOU WANT TO do what? No. No way!"

It was early January 2013, and the year was starting well. We had the cutest house in Aylmer, Quebec. We had neighbours we loved. I was working part time at my children's school and slowly building my freelance writing career. I had a group of friends who had kids the same age. My parents lived three blocks away.

And now my spouse had just announced that we should move back to Kanata, Ontario. There were a variety of reasons: It meant no more forty-five-minute commutes to work across the bridge in Ottawa. It meant lower provincial taxes. It meant English as the primary language, which would make accessing services a lot easier for my anglophone family members. Most importantly, it meant better access to mental health services for our middle child, who was riddled with inexplicable anxiety and depression. (That apple hadn't fallen far from the tree.)

When we left Kanata nearly two decades earlier, we had sworn never to return. Now my partner wanted to leave a community where I finally felt accepted and settle in a place where I felt anything but. I didn't want to go back to a place where the line was so clearly drawn between being a part of society and being shunned by it.

"But we're not going back to that," came my spouse's retort. "It's different now, more diverse and relaxed than it used to be. And we're not kids anymore, Amanda. We have a family too. We'll fit in."

"So we'll be just like them and that's how we'll fit in?" I shot back. "Great."

"I can't live here anymore. I've given it fourteen years and two houses. I'm just not happy."

"Oh, my husband isn't happy!" I said with mock surprise. "Well, there's a shocker." I walked out of the room with frustrated tears in my eyes. Why stay for the whole show? I knew how it ended anyway. We were moving.

I had some specific criteria that needed to be met for this move to take place: four bedrooms with a garage, easy walking distance to stores and at least one coffee shop, good schools and public transit for the kids, and a neighbourhood that was older and full of trees and parks. But it couldn't be pretentious. I wanted relaxed and diverse, just as I was promised, with weeds on lawns. We found it.

So guess what? We bought a house in Kanata.

Our realtor walked us through the home with our kids in tow. It was a private sale, so we warned our offspring not to act interested, even if they were. "Poker faces," I said sternly.

Five minutes into the tour, they were arguing loudly over

who would get which bedroom. The homeowner smiled knowingly. We put in an offer the next morning.

Our realtor took a picture of us on the day we signed the
papers. It looks like the most heteronormative scene of all
time: a husband and wife standing in front of a house in late
winter, holding each other and smiling excitedly. A new life! A
new beginning!

Oh, if only we'd known how true that would be.

—

I had to admit that Kanata wasn't awful. While I was sad to leave
the comforts of Aylmer, my social media presence made getting
established elsewhere a lot easier. I had mentioned on Twitter
that we were moving, and before long, we had a thriving community of friends. Sarah invited me over to talk neighbourhoods
before we got serious about putting in an offer anywhere.
Stephanie met me at the local Starbucks after we moved in and
became my first friend within walking distance.

Moving schools was arguably the hardest part. We had been a
South Hull Elementary family for more than a decade, with our
last child starting kindergarten shortly after our first went off to
high school. As a mom who worked and volunteered at the school,
I knew everyone. I sat on parent council. I attended nearly every
event. When our kids were struggling—especially our middle
one—I knew exactly who to talk to.

"He's having a bad day," I would say, and the admin staff
would nod in understanding. When we needed support, they provided it. One day, after my middle child flat-out refused to get
dressed or go to school, I walked in carrying said child in one arm
and a bag of clothing in the other, set both down in the front office

and said, "He's all yours." I didn't worry about being judged. By then, they understood that I had simply maxed out my nice-mom quota after many mornings just like that one.

But now I had gone from a school where I was on a first-name basis with everyone to one where I knew nobody. Each day, I would walk through the field to pick up the two younger kids and watch as other parents gathered together in groups to chat. Nobody said hello.

Well, that wouldn't do.

One day, I saw a notice on the front office wall introducing that year's parent council. One of the faces was familiar. Allison was the chair, and she was one of the few parents I had spoken to during a field trip not long before. She was funny and chatty, and I knew what I had to do.

I was now in my late thirties, and life experience had afforded me a bit more confidence. I hunted Allison down in the school-yard and mustered up the courage to walk up to her while we waited for the bell to ring.

"Hi," I said. "I don't know if you remember me from the museum trip, but my name is Amanda. I saw that you're the parent council chair, and I figured we should be friends. No one will give me the time of day here, and that's too bad because I'm pretty great."

Sunny, funny and charming. This girl still had it.

"Wonderful," said Allison, meeting my sassiness with an equal dose of her own. "Because I'm pretty great too."

We were friends from that moment on.

Allison introduced me to the rest of the parents on the coun-cil. They were a friendly bunch, eager to make school fundraisers wildly successful and have a good time while doing so. I began attending meetings and volunteering as frequently as possible. I bagged popcorn, parcelled out subs, sold movie tickets and raffled off cakes. It was a great way to get a good sense of the school culture and meet other families.

As I watched the kids start to settle into their new routines—the younger ones in grades one and six, and Aerik in grade ten at the high school down the road—I breathed a sigh of relief. There. We had successfully made the move, and my fears of what awaited us in Kanata were unfounded.

This was our new normal. We fit in here.

Well, at least some of us were fitting in. One of our kids wasn't settling into our new life as easily as the others and was, in fact, struggling in a way preteen me would have related to.

"I don't understand what's going on with him," I said to my mom on the phone. "I thought changing schools would help. A new neighbourhood, new friends, a fresh start, you know? But I can't get him out of bed again today. I'm at my wits' end."

Our eleven-year-old, the Most Planned Baby in the Universe, was inching toward a crisis. Anxiety had always been an issue, but it had taken on a crippling form, coupled with depression. Basic things like getting out of bed were impossible most mornings, and school attendance was poor. Hell, *life* attendance was poor.

Meltdowns had been a regular occurrence for years, but they were now becoming an almost daily event. They came out of nowhere, erupted over inconsequential things and put us all on edge. Objects were thrown and doors slammed, and our other two kids would disappear into their rooms, frightened and upset. Our middle child's screams were so loud that we had to shut the windows to contain the noise. (I even approached the neighbours on either side to let them know our child was dealing with mental health issues, not abuse. Thankfully, they were understanding.) At other times, anxiety would take the form of immobilization. If school felt overwhelming, there was no coaxing our preteen out of bed. At eleven and nearing a hundred pounds, the days of underarm pajama drop-offs were behind us.

Therapy wasn't helping. We had tried several different specialists over the years, from social workers at our local community resource centre to a world-renowned child psychologist. Nobody could dig deep enough to unearth the core issues. We also worked on improving nutrition and sleep habits and more exercise. At various times, we tried being firmer or more permissive. We created rigid schedules or took more a laissez-faire approach. Nothing worked.

At least there were more options available now that we had moved, and we were using nearly all of them. When our child threatened self-harm, we went to the children's hospital for emergency help. Because we didn't have a family physician yet, we visited every walk-in clinic we could find until one doctor referred us to a pediatrician who specialized in mental health. We had regular communication with the teachers, administrators and support staff, who worked hard to make school a positive experience. We had a therapist who was an expert in anxiety. We were administering antidepressants under the close supervision of the new pediatrician. Still, nothing seemed to be working.

"It's hard when our kids are hurting," my mom said as I cried to her on the phone. "I remember it well with you."

SEVEN

catalyst

TUESDAY, FEBRUARY 25, 2014, was the eve of Pink Shirt Day—a day to flash some pink at school to fight homophobia, transphobia and bullying of all kinds. Being my usual last-minute self, I took the kids to the store after dinner to find them something to wear. We searched the racks and kept coming up short. Everyone was getting frustrated.

"They don't have any pink shirts anywhere," my seven-year-old said, sounding flustered.

"You're right," I agreed. The boys' section was a muted wasteland of blues, browns and blacks. "I'm not finding any either."

"It's stupid!" he replied, a little too loudly. "Boys can like pink too. It's just a colour! I like pink, okay? It's nice. I should be able to wear it if I want to."

"You're right," I said again. "Isn't it weird how we separate colours by gender? It doesn't make any sense. Boys can wear pink, buddy. It's not a big deal. Don't let anyone tell you otherwise. You wear what you want, okay?"

"Well, *yeah*," he replied, as if I had just said something extremely obvious.

We eventually found one vivid extra-small pink shirt in the women's department and a light pink golf shirt in the men's section for his older sibling. *There!* I thought. *Both boys have shirts, and you are not the worst mother ever. Oh, and you even busted some long-standing gender stereotypes!*

I felt like a great mom that night—to my seven-year-old.

But there was someone else listening to that conversation who needed to hear what I had said even more than he did.

—

"Honey, you need to read this. Right now," my spouse said.

I was sitting at the desk in our bedroom after the pink-shirt escapade, trying to finish up a school project—*my* school project. Grade eleven English—Shakespeare Analysis, to be exact.

After moving back to Kanata, I had enrolled in an online program through a local adult high school. The fact that I didn't have a diploma was keeping me up at night. I didn't feel independent or accomplished, and I wanted to fix that. So now I spent my days writing parenting articles to pay the bills and my evenings writing essays on the symbolism in *Hamlet*. It was short-term pain for what I hoped would be long-term gain.

I pulled my eyes away from my large screen and focused on the smaller one on the phone being handed to me. On it was an email from our eleven-year-old, sent a few minutes earlier. All thoughts of *Hamlet* immediately fell away.

Please don't be angry.

Please try to understand.

I am a girl trapped in a boy's body.

My vision narrowed to a point and fixed solely on the words in front of me.

More than anything, I want to be a girl.

Please help me.

Don't come into my room until you've had a chance to calm down and think about it.

I love you. Please help me.

I immediately flashed to a day a few years before, when my mom and I were cleaning the playroom at the old house. It was as messy as a playroom for three kids could be, and I was grateful for the help. I put the TV on in the background while we dug in, and in short order, we both found ourselves captivated by a talk show featuring a family with a transgender child. The young girl was in a dress, her hair long and shiny, and she was truly indistinguishable from other girls her age. The large screen behind her kept flashing "before" photos, where she sported a more masculine haircut and clothing.

"I've always known I was a girl," the child said to the talk show host.

The audience members were not quiet in their judgment. People spat comments into the microphone like "What you're doing to your son is awful!" and "You're confusing him!" All the while, they were glaring at the mother. (It was always the mother.) The rest of the audience clapped, growing louder and angrier with each statement.

The host, while making a show of calming the audience, was demonstrating clear biases against the family. I felt for the mother, and especially for the young girl.

"This is so sad," my mom said.

"I don't really understand it," I replied, not taking my eyes off the screen. "I mean, is that kid old enough to know? Is it some kind of chemical imbalance? I just feel bad for the whole family."

"I knew a boy who was absolutely a girl," my mom said. "Everyone knew it. I think his parents even knew it. But those were different times. There was no way he could be anything but a boy."

In raising a child like that, and being advocates for her so publicly, the parents on the talk show exhibited a level of strength and self-confidence I couldn't imagine.

"You know," I said, going back to sorting toys during a commercial break, "I've been through a lot with my kids. But I don't know if I could handle that. It's too much." I was glad that girl had those parents instead of us. We wouldn't know what to do.

And now here we were, and as predicted, I didn't know what to do. I was still taking in the words on the screen, my thoughts coming faster than I could process them.

I had a son, didn't I? That's what I had believed from the moment the ultrasound technologist showed us what was between our baby's legs. I thought it was that simple. I thought we were raising a boy.

How did I miss this? How did I not see it coming? What kind of mother overlooks the clues that her child doesn't feel like the boy she thought she had?

I was in a parenting situation I had no clue how to handle. I was completely out of my depth. My head was spinning, and I found it hard to breathe.

I flashed back to the week when my son—or perhaps, my *daughter*—came home upset after school.

"They said the game is for girls only," my heartbroken child cried, pulling off a camouflage-patterned hoodie and slumping into a kitchen chair. It was spring, and the Japanese lilac in the front yard was in full bloom in the window. "I don't understand why they don't want to be my friends anymore."

"Sweetie, I'm sure they still want to be your friends," I said, taking a small hand, which was rough and dry from a hard winter. Eczema had always been a problem. Rubbing lotion into the rough spots was an easy way to soothe the pain. But I didn't know how to soothe *this* kind of pain. How could I explain that grade three is usually the time when kids who used to play together start to split by gender, and that the line in the sand would only continue to widen? Having nearly all girls as friends, my child was going to feel this division deeply.

The next day, I got a phone call from a neighbour. "My daughter asked your son if they could just hang out after school and not at recess," she said. "She wants to play with the other girls, and he keeps trying to join them." Apparently, it wasn't going well. "It's nothing personal," the neighbour added. "My daughter likes him. It's just that the other girls are giving her a hard time, and it's affecting her friendships at school. Maybe he has some other boys he can play with?"

My heart had hurt that day. Now it hurt even more as I held my son's—no, my daughter's—coming-out email in my hand. I was still in shock, running a million thoughts through my head as I tried to sort out what else this stay-at-home, parent-council, motherhood-is-the-one-thing-I-do-well person had missed all these years. And what incomprehensible damage had been done to my child because of it.

"What are we going to do?" my spouse asked.

I handed back the phone with the email on it and took a few purposeful breaths to try to steady my thoughts. We looked at each other with concern.

A transgender child. My head was stuffed so full of questions I couldn't think. Can kids even be transgender, I wondered, or is it something else? How do you find out? What's the parenting protocol for this? My anxiety was flaring up and making me physically ill. This was big. Too big.

Anxiety and I go way back, and I've learned a few tricks for when I start feeling overwhelmed. One is to remove all the unknowns causing stress and brain clutter so I can examine what I do know. And here's what I knew for sure in that moment:

- Our child had just told us something critical.
- Our child needed our support.
- The love we had for our child was unconditional.

Stripping it down to the bare facts didn't make the issue any less complicated, but it did make clear what we should do next.

"We love our child," I replied. "And we figure the rest out later. Let's go in there."

We got up and walked across the hall to a bedroom containing one very frightened—and very brave—kid.

"Hey, sweetie," I said. "Can we come in?"

The only answer came in sobs.

We opened the door and crawled into bed with our middle child, who was shaking and inconsolable.

"We love you no matter what," we said again and again. And when tears were the only replies, we filled the spaces where words should go with more reassurances. "We don't care if you're a boy or a girl," we said. "All we care about is that you're happy. We'll figure this out together, okay? We're so glad you told us what's going on."

We told our child that things would be okay. That *she* would be okay.

EIGHT

unlearning

BUT THINGS WERE not okay. *I* was not okay.

After a while, I gently excused myself from our child's room and stepped out into the hallway. That was when I lost my composure. Not because my kid was likely trans, but because the revelation had just blown away my delicate house of cards.

Until that moment, parenting was the one thing I knew I did well. That no longer rang true. I was ill-equipped to deal with this, and I realized that could seriously harm my child. I was not the mother on that talk show stage. I was not nearly that strong, capable or informed. I was flying blind, and I was sure her other parent was too.

I needed to find out what being a transgender child meant. I grabbed my computer and typed in the words "transgender children." Thousands of search results popped up. I wondered what it would have been like to go looking for information on transgender issues before the invention of search engines. What would you do? See your doctor? Go to your local library?

Thankfully, my work as a freelance writer had led me on some deep journalistic diving expeditions, and I knew enough to stick to well-known, established medical sites and reputable LGBTQ organizations. I figured that if anyone knew how to help trans people, it would be other trans people and those who worked closely with them.

I also reached out to two key friends that night: a sex educator whose practice focuses on helping families talk about sexual health, and a social worker specializing in LGBTQ clients. Both women responded quickly with information on how to support our child. They sent lists of local resources, websites and recommended books, and they offered suggestions on what to do next, like asking our kid what pronouns we should use.

"Ask what pronouns we should be using?" I whispered as I read the reply, confusion all over my face. "Really?"

I had always known this young person as a boy. We had always used "he" and "him." The idea of using anything else felt foreign. The idea of letting someone choose their own pronouns felt even more so.

But I was going to need to get over my discomfort. Because my late-night research had also revealed the abysmal statistics on outcomes for trans youth. This extremely vulnerable population carries high rates of depression, anxiety, self-harm and suicide. Trans kids are more likely to face discrimination, harassment, bullying and assault. LGBTQ young people are disproportionately represented in the homeless population, finish high school less often and have a harder time finding work. The world doesn't understand or accept them, the websites seemed to say, and this makes their lives exceptionally harder.

I don't know what suicidal ideation is like for other people. I only know that for teenage me, the idea crept into my mind slowly. When it first entered, I quickly escorted it to the door. But the more it showed up, the more exhausting it became to send it away. I would let it linger. Before long, it took over my thoughts. Depression is smooth, subtle and conniving.

By fourteen, I had endured years of bullying, the two fire-related attacks and a sexual assault. I had pushed away the few good friends I had with lies, anger or avoidance. I yelled at my siblings and swore at my parents, which allowed me to spend long hours alone in my room. There, I could self-harm with razors whenever the emotional pain became too much. Depression isolates us through any means necessary.

I planned my death for a night when my parents were going out. I knew they would be home shortly after I was gone, and well before any of my siblings woke up. I didn't want my brothers and sister at home without supervision, but I also didn't want anyone to stop me from freeing myself of pain. I thought that life would never get better. That I would always be the butt of someone's joke. That I would never succeed at anything. By ending my life, I told myself, I was doing everyone a favour. I wouldn't be a burden to my family. But mostly, I wouldn't have to suffer anymore.

I wasn't scared of dying. In fact, I welcomed it and felt relieved to be on the other side of doubt. But as I prepared to say a final goodbye to the world I hated, the phone rang, loud and startling, echoing throughout the house. My eyes shot open. It rang again. I thought about not answering it, but I didn't want the noise to wake my siblings.

When I picked up the receiver and said hello, a deep, soft voice I had never heard before asked to speak to Amanda.

"It's me," I said, a little confused. "Who's this?"

"My name is Kevin," said the voice. "I'm Amelia's boyfriend. She asked me to call you. Did she let you know? I hope I'm not bothering you."

Amelia was an acquaintance at my new school. She had a warm, empathetic smile and fiery red hair. That day, she had noticed the fresh cuts I was trying to hide and took me aside to ask me about them. I confided in her that I wasn't feeling great, and that hurting myself was a way to let the pain out. She asked if I wanted to talk to her boyfriend. "He's been there," she said. "Maybe he could help."

I agreed because I wanted to appease her—did I mention that Amelia was really nice?—but I knew I probably wouldn't be alive to talk to him. I was going to die that night, after all. And yet here he was, calling a stranger out of the blue and being quite prompt about it.

Kevin told me his story of struggle and how he had overcome what was the darkest period of his young life. He asked about my own struggles. I hesitated for only a moment. What did I have to lose at this point? I told him everything, from Zenji to the drug-dealer rapist, and he listened carefully through it all.

"Want to meet up tomorrow?" he asked. We went to different schools but lived only a quick bus ride from each other. "You seem like someone I'd like to be friends with. And it sounds like you need someone who gets it."

That is how Kevin saved my life—by having me hold on one more day. When I met him the following afternoon, we hit it off immediately and understood each other on a deep level. For the next few months, Kevin became my rock and one of my closest friends. Even when his family moved to Winnipeg, I knew I could always call him. That was the love I needed to get me through. There's a sealed-up crack in my foundation with his initials on it. Years later, I would find him online and thank him for saving my life.

———

Memories of Kevin and my own suicidal thoughts made my fears for my child grow bigger. I didn't know what it felt like to be trans, but I did know what it was like to go through a lot of the same issues: self-harm, suicidal ideation, depression, anxiety, harassment, bullying and assault. I had also been to rehab and lived in shelters, and I was just now trying to finish my high school education after several failed attempts. I knew what it was like not to be accepted by those around you, even if for different reasons.

I had been a parent for nearly my entire adult life. In that time, I had worked to keep my children far away from the pain I had experienced when I was younger. I wanted them to have a better life, a less rickety foundation. But now, faced with the news of who this child really was, all I could see was a life fraught with hazards. I could lose her to the very things that had nearly swallowed me too.

No. That would *not* be her life. I wouldn't let that happen. If this was the thorny path the world was going to put at her feet, I was going to walk hand in hand with her, carrying a giant machete. A fire had been lit inside me. Now I know how activism is born.

My spouse left our daughter's bedroom about an hour after I did and found me reading an article on medical support options for transgender children.

"Learning anything interesting?"

"A lot," I said. "Too much. I can't believe this is happening. I'm scared."

"I know. Me too. But it explains a lot, doesn't it? The outbursts, the depression, the anxiety—all of it makes more sense now."

"It does. I just can't believe we didn't see it until now." Guilt squeezed my heart.

"It's a hard thing to see if someone doesn't tell you, Amanda—especially if they're doing their best to hide it."

I would kick myself a few more times before I finally got the guilt out of my system. But I realized it was time to focus on what our child needed from that moment on, not what she might have benefited from earlier.

It was time to go forward.

Our daughter was, understandably, too upset and vulnerable to go to school the next day. I made use of the time at home, just the two of us, to gently dig deeper into what had prompted her to send that email. She told me that she had typed "Why do I feel like a girl when I'm a boy?" into a search engine a few weeks back, her stomach in knots. She was desperately seeking answers to long-standing questions.

For years, her life had felt . . . *wrong*. Just wrong. There was no other way to describe it. But whenever we asked her what was behind her chronic melancholy, she didn't know how to tell us. She didn't have the language to describe the level of discomfort she felt in her life and her body.

She reminded me of a recent conversation. "Did you know we gave you my favourite boy's name?" I had asked. "It's Irish. You're named after a saint, which is kind of funny, since we're not religious. But it's a beautiful name. Strong and masculine, but also poetic. It suits you."

No, it hurt her, she explained to me now. That name, written everywhere—from the front of her bedroom door to the inside of her backpack, scrawled on every craft and quiz brought home from school—cut her to the core. Being called by that name in class or even across the dining room table made her want to cry. That hadn't always been the case, but as she slowly became aware that she wasn't a boy, she started to view the name as a shackle to a life that didn't fit.

"You made a big deal out of having three boys," she explained to me. "You wrote about us in your blog a lot, and you seemed so proud of it."

She was right. I regularly joked about the chaos a trifecta of testosterone would bring upon our household in the teen years. I considered the banged-up walls and stained furniture a badge of honour when I talked about my family. I hung ornaments on the Christmas tree with all their names, bought them matching pajamas and had them pose for pictures. "I just love my boys so much!" I would exclaim, hugging them all.

"I didn't want to say you were wrong," she explained to me now. "I was scared you would be disappointed."

Her being a boy was a part of my identity. But it wasn't a part of hers.

Now puberty had hit. My child was experiencing changes that were counter to what she knew about herself. She wanted breasts and instead was getting a more defined jaw. She wanted hips but was getting dark hair on her upper lip instead.

"I had to know why I felt like a girl when everyone else thought I was a boy. It was so confusing, Mom."

She didn't know how to have that conversation with us. She didn't know how to explain it to the few friends she had. So she asked the internet, and it provided answers.

Transgender. She had never heard the word before, but it came up time and time again in her searches. In 2014, the voices of trans people were emerging in their own community. She found articles and blog posts from older transgender people who wrote about why they'd needed to start living life as their true selves. She found YouTube videos from trans kids who explained what it felt like to be allowed to grow up as the gender they really are.

"I finally had an answer," she said. "But a lot of the stories about coming out are so scary."

"How so?" I asked.

"A lot of kids get yelled at or kicked out or abused. And some get put into therapy to try to make them stop thinking they're trans."

Conversion—or reparative—therapy. I had heard of this harmful practice used on gay people, and it sickened me. Surely she knew we would never do that to her?

"But I didn't know that," she said. "A lot of kids thought their parents would be supportive, but they weren't at all. I was worried."

As she discovered who she was, she wondered how we would take it. Would we understand, or would we try to shove her back in the closet, as many other families had done?

"I just needed a sign you were going to be okay," she said. "And then we went shopping for pink shirts, and you said the things you did about gender stereotypes. That's when I knew I could tell you."

I had to take a deep breath to stop myself from crying. Here I was, wracked with guilt, and I didn't need to be. Without realizing it, I had created a safe place for my child. Isn't that what all parents should do?

The email she wrote, beautifully crafted for a child her age, took over an hour to compose. She wanted to do it right—to make us understand what it was like to be transgender. At eleven, the words "a girl trapped in a boy's body" were the best she could come up with. It wasn't a perfect description, but she hoped it would get the job done.

After writing, rewriting and editing it for what felt like an eternity, she hovered her cursor over the Send button. This decision could not be undone. If it didn't go well, there was nothing she could do. She would be at the mercy of our judgment.

"So I took a deep breath, hit Send, turned off the screen and crawled into bed, terrified."

"I'm sorry you felt so scared," I said. "I hope we put your fears to rest."

"You did," she replied. "Thank you. I think things are going to start getting better now."

—

It was time to get to work. I called everyone I could think of. There was a clinic at the Children's Hospital of Eastern Ontario, or CHEO, that had gender identity specialists—whatever that meant. There was someone who worked with trans adults at one of the downtown health centres who might know of additional resources. There was a trans person working out of Family Services Ottawa who was supposed to be putting together a support group for parents of trans children.

I spoke to everyone in a single day. Now that I've known all these people for a few years, I recognize how improbable it was to get even one of them on the phone that day, let alone all of them. Their calmness, reassurance and insight were exactly what I needed in that moment. They were people who either had been through the early stages of transition themselves or had worked with many people who had. I frantically scribbled notes as they talked. This was a crash course on a topic I never thought I'd be studying.

It was a productive first day. We were invited to the new parents' group the following week and put on a waiting list to see someone at the hospital's gender diversity clinic. Most importantly, I was assured by everyone I spoke to that we were on the right path. "Following your child's lead in these situations is critical," they told me again and again. Good thing that was happening.

I mean, sort of. Well, most of the time.

Knowing what I know now, I would love to tell this story in a way that paints me in a better light. It would be great to say I immediately embraced my child's gender as legitimate and permanent. But that would be a lie. Humans make mistakes. Thankfully, we can also learn from those mistakes.

Some of what I did was right. I got over myself and asked what pronouns my child would like us to use. She asked that we use "she" and "her" in the house, but "he" and "him" outside of it, at least for the short term. Tricky but manageable. Admittedly, calling the child I had known as my son for eleven years by female pronouns felt awkward at first. But so had the first time I did squats at the gym, and now I do them without thinking. Pronouns, I figured, were a lot like squats: I would trip all over them at first, but they would get easier with practice.

I was stuck on the permanency of her gender identity, however. I wondered if someone her age could make such a big proclamation and mean it in a "forever" kind of way. A lot of kids try on different labels for size. Maybe she was just trying this out, you know? And if that was the case, how far down this path did we want to go?

I tried to find what I thought were subtle ways of bringing this up with her. As it turns out, I wasn't very subtle at all.

"I'm just wondering," I said one day, "and I mean, I fully support you in who you are, but I'm wondering how long you've felt this way."

"A long time, Mom," she replied.

"Well, it's just that I'm reading this book right now that was recommended to me—and I tracked down the last copy in the city, by the way, so you know I'm serious about learning!—and it says most transgender children show signs early on. Like saying they don't feel right in their bodies, or insisting their gender isn't what everyone thinks it is."

"Uh-huh." She knew exactly where I was going with this.

"But you didn't do that," I continued. "You weren't trying on dresses or wanting to grow your hair long. You never argued when people referred to you as a boy. Sure, you liked a lot of things that are deemed more feminine, like dance classes and playing restaurant and that brief Hannah Montana phase. But you never said anything. You seemed fine."

"I wasn't fine, though," she replied. "Why do you think I never wanted to go to school? Why do you think I had such a hard time making friends after the girls stopped playing with me? I just didn't know what it was for a while, and I didn't have the words to tell you two."

"Okay, but—"

She cut me off. "It's not a phase, Mom. I know that's what

you're getting at. *It's not*. This is who I am. I already told you. Stop questioning it."

I wish I could say I did stop, but there would be a few more times. I was grasping at straws, hoping beyond hope this wasn't happening. Society makes life hard on trans people, and I didn't want my child to face a mountain of challenges. The Most Planned Baby in the Universe had thrown the plans out the window without warning, and I was understandably worried for her. But that doesn't excuse my incessant questioning in those first few days. Later, she would tell me how much those conversations hurt her. I will carry that for the rest of my life. But more importantly, she'll carry it, and that's so unfair.

At the same time, I was also struggling with something common to a lot of us in my generation: ingrained transphobia. I knew very little about the trans community. Until our child came out, I didn't really need to know, and I didn't take the time to learn. I had no ill will against the community, and I firmly believed people have the right to be who they are. But I was also raised in a time and a society that mocked, misunderstood and feared trans people. This left me with some big misconceptions, even if I didn't realize it.

The movies and shows I had grown up on were chock full of transphobia. Trans people were the antagonists, the deranged, the deceptive or the butt of the joke. They were unstable geniuses with mommy issues or perverted tricksters trying to fool the ones they were seducing. They were fetishized, ridiculed and never painted in a good light. They were also never played by actual trans people.

Like a lot of folks my age, I didn't know any out trans people who could dispel those harmful myths. All I knew was what I saw on the screen or heard about in conversations with others who weren't trans. I spent a lifetime with only those negative examples. But in 2014, the media was beginning to turn its attention to the trans community in an educational way, spotlighting people like Chaz Bono and Janet Mock. Hollywood was just starting to cast real trans people in more positive roles. I had watched Laverne Cox in *Orange Is the New Black* and learned more about actual trans issues from one episode featuring her character's backstory than I had from all previous negative media representations combined.

Like racism or homophobia, transphobia can take a lifetime to acknowledge and unlearn. But this is especially important to do when you're raising a trans child who needs your unwavering support. I needed to unlearn at warp speed.

I knew this was critical the first time I took her shopping for clothes to wear around the house. She seemed delighted by the fabrics, and commented shyly on the colours and patterns she liked most. I should have been pleased for her and excited to experience a "first" with my daughter. Instead, everything about that day felt wrong, but I couldn't put my finger on why. I was clouded by all I had learned, all the misconceptions I had internalized throughout my life. She was happy, and I should have been happy. Instead, I was fighting the idea that this was a child who was just trying to be herself.

I knew I had some work to do, and I had better do it quickly. Because if I didn't, she would be the one to pay the price.

—

"Have you thought of a name?"

I had come to see her in her room for a chat the day after we went shopping. It had occurred to me that in order to get comfortable with the changes, I had to immerse myself in them. I wanted to get to know my daughter *as* my daughter. Sure, she was technically still the same person, but I could already sense there was a whole lot more to her that had been locked away for a long time. There was a little flower blooming in front of my eyes, and I wanted to know if it had a name.

For the first few days, we avoided using any name as much as possible; the old one caused her too much pain, and a new one would have raised questions with those we hadn't told, including her siblings. Other than both sets of grandparents, the experts I had talked to and a handful of close friends, nobody but me and my spouse knew what was going on. In my research, I had also read that it was important not to "out" trans people. My daughter would have to tell her friends and family herself or give me permission to do it for her. This was her journey and I was doing my best to be a good co-pilot: gathering information, making suggestions, but not taking over. We would go at her speed.

"I have some ideas for names," she said, and began listing them off.

I didn't like any of them. I opened my mouth to say so, and a little voice inside me screamed: *Co-pilot, co-pilot, co-pilot!*

Deep breath. "Those are great ideas!" I said. "Let's put a pin in them and maybe check out some others as well. Did you know I thought I was going to have a girl when I was pregnant with you?"

"You did have a girl," she said matter-of-factly.

Argh! Proper language! Ingrained transphobia! Rampant unintentional assholeness!

Another deep breath. "Right! Yes, of course. I didn't mean it that way. What I meant is that I thought we had a boy, but it turns out we had a girl all along, which is amazing! I'm so excited!" That wasn't a lie. My fears had put a damper on that excitement, but it was still there. Even though I had been happy being a mom to what I thought were three boys, a part of me had always longed to have a daughter. This discovery was unexpected and came about in a way I could never have predicted.

She smiled. She could see I was trying.

"What names did you have picked out for me?" she asked.

This was a bonding moment. I could feel it.

"Well," I began, "we both really liked the name Meghan."

"Gross. That sounds like an eighties name."

I opened my mouth—and promptly shut it again. *Co-pilot, co-pilot!* Also, it was true. It *was* an eighties name.

"Okay, how about Annika? That's a little trendier."

She cringed. "Like the Star Wars kid?"

"No, that's Anakin."

"They sound a lot alike. People would call me the Star Wars kid."

"Fine. Any other ideas?" I asked in that so-you-think-you-can-name-yourself tone.

"I like the name Kerri. K-E-R-R-I."

"Kerri Knox? KK? Isn't that how people reply to each other in texts now?"

"Oh my God, Mom." She rolled her eyes at me. "Not for the last five years."

And that's when I saw it. Really saw it. That eye roll was the exact one I used to give to my own mother when she said something I *clearly* knew more about. My daughter was behaving exactly like I had.

"Another name we really liked was Alexis."

"Alexis," she said, mulling it over. "Alexis Kerri Knox. Yeah, I like it. It suits me."

And just like that, my daughter had a name.

"I think for now, though, we should just call me Alex when we're out in public."

Alex. Alexis. My daughter. Cool.

—

"Are we telling your brothers today?" I asked the following afternoon. This was the flight plan she had come up with. As her co-pilot, I was simply checking in.

"Yeah, I think we should," Alexis said. "I don't like keeping things from them."

I could see she was nervous. While we had quickly rallied around her, her siblings might not. They were seventeen and seven years old. I figured Aerik could get to a place of acceptance relatively quickly, but Jackson might struggle and would certainly have plenty of questions.

We sat them down in the living room after school, and Alexis started to talk. She told them everything, from how sad and confused she had been to when she realized she was trans. She asked for their understanding and support. At the end, Aerik gave her a big hug and said he loved her no matter what. Jackson sat on the couch, lost in thought.

"Wait a minute," he said, the wheels turning in his mind. "Let me get this straight: everyone thought you were a boy, but inside you felt like a girl?"

"Yeah, that's about right," Alexis replied.

"Okay. Cool. I always wanted a sister, anyway." He gave her a hug too, and that was that.

I kept waiting for the other shoe to drop. I thought that maybe one of the boys would end up having a harder time with it. That never happened.

The following day, I realized that Jackson had fully internalized this sister business when he ran upstairs to tattle on her and used her pronouns perfectly. "And then she hit me!" he yelled. "Alexis is such a jerk! She's the worst!"

I suppressed a grin as I listened, and he got mad that I wasn't taking his issues seriously. It's still one of my favourite stories to tell.

confrontation

IN THE FIRST few weeks after Alexis came out, when she was at her most vulnerable, I acted like her shield—and often felt quite alone in it. I had taken the lead on all things transition-related: gathering information, making appointments, talking to people I'd been allowed to share with, and regularly checking in with Alexis and her brothers. It was a big emotional load. My spouse, while seemingly supportive, remained a step removed from the process. I didn't understand why, but I also didn't have time to figure it out. It was a critical point in Alexis's life, and she needed to know she could count on us.

I focused my attention on carving out as many safe environments for her as possible. I called the dental office ahead of a scheduled cleaning and asked if they had ever worked with transgender patients before. They had, but not a child. Still, they were quick to switch her name and gender marker in their system. I spoke to her pediatrician prior to an upcoming appointment.

"I don't believe I have any other transgender patients in my practice," he said. "So this will be a learning opportunity for me."

It was a learning opportunity for many of us. Trans youth were not coming out at the rates they are today. The term "transgender" was still alien to, or at least misunderstood by, most people we spoke to outside of the medical community. For many of those people, Alexis was their first known point of contact with a trans-gender individual. There were some ignorant questions as people wrapped their minds around the concept, but the general reac-tion was kind. The many fears I had about Alexis living as herself were beginning to slip away. *Maybe*, I thought, *this will be easier than the disaster scenario my anxiety-riddled mind conjured up.*

But one of the biggest stresses in those first few weeks still remained: How were we going to handle telling people at school?

I had been learning how unique transition is for each person going through it. How, when and even *if* trans people present their true selves to the world depends on several factors, includ-ing personal preference, safety, support, finances, job security, family acceptance and access to medical care. Timelines vary widely. Some walk out the door fully expressing their gender right away, while others take slow and steady steps in that direction. And some never come out at all.

Now that she was getting more comfortable with the idea of being out, Alexis had made very clear that she needed to transi-tion socially as soon as possible, moving quickly from being perceived as a boy to living as a girl. She wanted to wear femi-nine clothing, grow her hair and be called by the right name and pronouns by everyone. She wanted to use the bathroom that matched her gender identity and be wholly accepted as "just one of the girls."

I wanted to make all this happen for her, but I wasn't sure how. At the time, our school board didn't have an official policy or any guidelines on how to support transgender kids. There was some training happening, but not all schools had received it. My stomach was in knots anticipating what the reaction would be.

I'd like to say that engaging the school was an easy process. But there were some initial bumps. After meeting with Alexis's very supportive teacher, I worked up the courage to talk to an administrator. It didn't go well. Concern clouded her face as I shared what our daughter had told us, and what had transpired in our discussions with the teacher.

She suggested that perhaps my child could wait until middle school the following year to transition, as this could be "easier." She wondered aloud if other parents would have an issue with the transition and worried about potential backlash. She asked me to refrain from talking about the situation with anyone else at the school and even sent a follow-up email stating that we were no longer to speak directly to the teacher—all concerns should go solely to the administrative staff. And although I consistently used Alexis's new pronouns, she kept using the old ones.

It was a very discouraging meeting. I felt no support in her words, only apprehension and misunderstanding. I searched for my own words to counter hers but couldn't find them. It was all too new, and I was feeling entirely too vulnerable. Everything I had feared about telling the school had come true in the span of ten minutes. I walked out of her office in a daze, went back to my car in the parking lot and burst into tears.

Too upset to drive, I called my mother instead. "This can't be the way it is," I cried. "How do I fight for her? I feel like the whole world is against us right now. I'm not strong enough for this, Mom. I can't fight like you."

"Amanda," she said calmly, "I know this is hard. Believe me, I know. But you *are* strong enough."

My mother knew how to fight for a child because she'd had to as well. Her fourth child, my brother Mike, was born with Down syndrome when I was eleven; my sister, Katie, was four; and my other brother, Charlie, was two. Michael was a beautiful baby with bright blue eyes and squishy little toes—a cherub in a Michelangelo painting. He was perfection, and you couldn't tell me otherwise.

One of our most striking family pictures was taken minutes after his birth, new life wrapped up in hospital blankets and held close by my mom, who looks on with a mixture of joy and sadness in her red, weepy eyes. Joy for having just given birth to a child she already loved, and sadness, I'm guessing, because she knew his life would be filled with challenges.

Mike had a host of medical issues and developmental delays, although we wouldn't know how much that extra chromosome would affect him until later. For a while, we didn't know if there would be a "later." We lived life one day, one new medical condition, one specialist appointment at a time. Mike's early years were especially frightening: pneumonia, partially collapsing lungs, infections, feeding tubes and a prediction that he wouldn't live a long life.

My parents were judged harshly for bringing a child with Down syndrome into the world when fetal test results had indicated the condition. I once overheard someone complain to my mom that the baby would burden the taxpayer by putting pressure on the province's public health-care system. My parents were chastised by more than one medical professional, both before and after

Mike was born, for not terminating the pregnancy. A grim picture was painted for his future: he would never walk, never talk, never achieve the hopes and dreams all parents have for their children.

I watched as my parents—and in particular, my mother—defended their decision. My mom would not bow to pressure or accept any of the dire predictions made by doctors. She was a fierce advocate from the minute she felt Mike kick inside her, and she insisted her son be treated with as much dignity and respect as any other child.

As someone who cared too much about what my peers thought of me, I admired her ability to ignore people's scorn. To her, Mike deserved the same opportunities as her other children, and she would do whatever she needed to make that happen. She set up a group called Integration Action, which lobbied the government and local school boards to integrate more special-needs children into regular classrooms. She felt it was beneficial for all kids to get to know and grow up with children with developmental disabilities. This, she hoped, would break down barriers and create a more inclusive world.

Today, thanks in large part to the work my mom did, my brother works for the federal government on Parliament Hill. He's respected by his colleagues and adored by everyone who meets him. Mike is a testament to how love and inclusion can make a meaningful difference.

My mother wasn't just my first glimpse into advocacy—she was a goddamned supernova.

Now, whimpering to her in my car outside of Alexis's school, I felt I'd never measure up. "I'm not strong enough, Mom. I froze up in there. It was awful. I didn't stand up for her. I couldn't get the words out. She needs better than I can give her."

"Listen to me," she said in her best mom voice. "If there's anyone who can advocate for her child, it's you. Remember that time Jackson was really sick and they turned you away at the hospital, saying it was nothing? What did you do?"

"I took him back in," I said, sniffling. At two, Jackson had fallen ill with some worrisome symptoms. I went to the ER twice—the second time with my mom in tow—before they took me seriously. He ended up being treated for a rare autoimmune issue called Kawasaki disease, and spent a week in hospital and several weeks recovering at home.

"Right," she said. "You wouldn't take no for answer. Have a good cry and get back up again. Don't let anyone push you around. *You're* the mother; she's *your* child. Nobody knows her better than you. You're going to make sure they give her what she needs. That's the attitude you have to go in with. Got it?"

"Got it," I said.

Moms are amazing.

—

A few days later, once I was calm again, I wrote an articulate email to that administrator, copying all the important people, to address my concerns about what had transpired. Then I stated clearly what I would like to see happen for Alexis on the school front. I made sure that everyone knew I fully understood my child's rights in the province of Ontario. I explained that Alexis would be dictating how quickly she transitioned at school—not them, me, or anyone else. I emphasized that I would be speaking directly to the teacher about Alexis, as I did with every other issue affecting my child.

It was March break, but I got a reply within hours. We set up a meeting with the appropriate staff to work out how to properly support Alexis in her transition. They all did a fantastic job from that moment on, including that administrator.

That was my first foray into advocacy as the mother of a trans-gender child, and while it was scary and gut-wrenching, it was also empowering. No small thanks to my own mom, I was starting to feel like the parent Alexis deserved.

Alexis's teacher, meanwhile, was in her final year before retirement and had never, to her knowledge, had a trans student before. But she jumped on board without hesitation. Her concern for Alexis was obvious. She asked her all the right questions: When would Alexis like to tell the other students? How would she go about doing that? What would she like help with? The teacher was a shining example of an educator willing to continue learning throughout her career.

The school had offered training on trans issues in the past, but the principal set up a new session for the staff so everyone would be up to date on the latest information. The office changed Alexis's name in the records system to reflect how she wanted to be addressed and what should go home on her report cards. The school had no change rooms—kids did gym in the clothes they wore from home—but it did have gendered washrooms. Because she was still early in her transition, Alexis didn't feel ready to use the girls' washroom, for fear of harassment and ridicule. But she didn't feel comfortable in the boys' washroom either. Ultimately, she was offered the use of a single-stall staff wash-room in the front office. On the surface, this seemed like a good idea, but she was often stopped and questioned by employees who didn't realize she was allowed to use it. Each time, she would have to explain that she had been given permission. Eventually, she stopped using the washroom during the day as much as possible.

Before all this, I had considered myself an aware person, liberal and open-minded. Now, I was amazed by how much I didn't know, and how many preconceived notions were in my head about issues I had no lived experience with. For years, I'd held strong opinions with nothing to back them up. Those are the most dangerous kind.

In 2011, a couple in the Toronto area made headlines by choosing to raise their baby without a gender. The parents and older siblings knew what anatomy the child had, but they weren't disclosing it to anyone. When Storm was old enough to declare a gender, friends and family would find out what that was. The press picked up the story, and it provoked international comment. Suddenly, everyone had an opinion on how baby Storm was being raised.

I wish I could go back far enough in my Facebook history to find the posts I wrote condemning that family. But to sum it up, I said something along the lines of how confusing and harmful this would be to the child. I said boys and girls are different, whether we want to acknowledge that or not. I said it's fine to let girls do more masculine things and boys do more feminine things, but we should call them what they are.

Basically, I said all the same things people like to say to me on social media these days.

Funny, that.

A few months after Alexis came out, a friend who had been on the other side of that debate and spoke up in defence of the parents posted an update on the family to my Facebook feed and asked if my opinions had changed. Of course they had. I now had a living, breathing example of how rigid and wrong I had been about gender.

In the update, the family stated they simply wanted Storm to figure things out without any expectations, so they removed those expectations entirely. I have no idea if this method is the best way, but I do know what *didn't* work for one of my own kids: stuffing her into a gender box from the day she was born, based entirely on what was between her legs.

My long-held beliefs about a lot of things started to slip away. I had once been the person arguing on parenting boards about breastfeeding, not sleep-training your baby and a host of other hotly debated topics. I was the captain of Team Righteous, and I had no problem telling others they were wrong for not doing everything the way I did. I likely hurt a lot of feelings and caused a lot of discomfort. But I didn't think of that. I only thought about being right.

Being right meant being a good mom. Being a good mom meant I didn't feel like a failure in this one area of my life. Now I realized how wrong I had been about a big issue, however, and I had no choice but to own it. The evidence was right in front of me, in the form of an eleven-year-old girl I didn't know I had.

I had spent years trying to prop up my unstable sense of self. Everything I had built in life—my confidence, my career, my relationships, my parenting—rested upon shaky ground. I felt so insecure that I had to defend my position at all costs. I had to pick a hill and die on it if need be. Because if I wasn't right about this one issue, perhaps I was wrong about everything. And if I was wrong about everything, maybe I—Amanda—was wrong. Unworthy of love. Complete personal failure.

I guarded my opinions and my ego fiercely until the walls caved in on my foundation. Bruised and sheepish, I had to dig myself out, dust myself off and do better in the future. This ability to push through, even when it feels awful, is called resiliency. It's something I had been cultivating for a long time without even realizing it.

It's good thing too, because I was about to get a lesson on what happens when you're the parent on the other side of all that judgment.

—

Allison, the parent council chair I'd befriended in the school-yard with my awesome speech about how awesome I am, became the ally I didn't realize I needed. It turned out that the administrator who had worried about the reactions of other parents to Alexis's transition was not entirely wrong. Parents can be a bigger problem than kids when it comes to accep-tance. We're a full generation behind in our learning and exposure to diversity.

Some of the people in my generation were learning new things, but many were lagging—often by stubborn choice. As word of Alexis's transition spread to people we knew at school, a few objected. One previously friendly woman who'd regularly attended parent council events with me abruptly stopped acknowledging my existence. And I don't mean she would say a frosty hello and then move on. I mean that when I was talking to someone we both knew, Judgmental Mom would walk up to us, turn toward the other person with her back to me and start chatting as if I weren't even there.

Judgmental Mom did know I existed, however, because she told mutual friends that my spouse and I were damaging Alexis by allowing her to live as a girl. She felt that it went against God's teachings, and that we were all unfortunate victims of a liberal agenda championed by the LGBTQ community. It wasn't our fault; we were just doing what the so-called experts were telling us to do. But what we were doing was wrong because those doctors and counsellors were victims too. They were being bullied by the same activists who were leading countless families astray.

I heard about her tirades on more than one occasion from people who'd witnessed them. Some would come to our defence, but it never changed her mind. She was convinced she was right. *Gee, that sounds terribly familiar, Amanda. Maybe that's what karma feels like.*

If not for a few wonderful women on the parent council, my family and I might have avoided school-related events entirely. But these women were determined to keep us a part of the school community, and they reminded us of upcoming events and openly demonstrated their support when we did come. They taught me what allies look like by always ensuring that we felt safe and welcomed whenever we stepped through the school doors.

When dealing with difficult people, I often think of that long-ago encounter with Sylvia in the grocery store. In that moment, I chose kindness. But I didn't do it for her. Hell, the girl set me on fire and showed absolutely no remorse, even years later! She didn't deserve my kindness. No, I did it for Aerik, who was young and watching my every move. And I did it for me because I wanted to walk away from that conversation feeling like I had done the right thing. I knew I'd have to live with whatever I said or did for the rest of my life.

I had lost some of that kindness over the following years, particularly while engaging with other parents online. When the smugness of those exchanges wore off, I always felt awful. But that moment with Sylvia reminded me that I wanted to be the mother Alexis, Aerik and Jackson deserved, especially now that we were facing increased scrutiny. It was time to go back to what felt good and lead the way with kindness.

So I didn't confront Judgmental Mom about her intolerance. I didn't berate her for what she said when I wasn't around, or for ignoring me when I was. Instead, I thought I would help her be more like Jesus, who seemed to be a guy she really looked up to. What would Jesus do? Well, if my Catholic school upbringing taught me anything, it's that the man had no issues hanging out with people his daddy considered sinners. We could help hone that quality!

Alexis was spending a lot of time with me back then. She knew I would be there to help correct any misgendering (using the wrong pronouns) or deadnaming (using her old name). I was still catching up in the learning department, but I had her back. I also knew that Judgmental Mom, as awful as she could be, would not openly mistreat or ignore Alexis. She did have some core values, and one of them seemed to be showing respect to kids.

Excellent.

Judgmental Mom and I often volunteered at school events. Movie night was coming up, and Alexis asked if she could come with me to help.

"I'd love for you to come," I said. "But I want you to know there's going to be someone there who thinks supporting you in transition is the wrong thing to do. She might not hide her views very well." This was a tough but important conversation to have. Transphobia was something Alexis would likely have to deal with to some degree for the rest of her life. Learning how to be around intolerant people was an important skill to master.

"Is this the woman I heard you talking about on the phone? The one who thinks you're bad parents?" she asked.

"Yes," I replied. Damn kids with ears. "But she mostly just ignores me."

"I'll tell her off if she does that," Alexis said defensively.

"I have a better idea." I smiled.

We arrived at movie night half an hour before the doors opened. Soon, kids would be pouring in with their parents. The volunteer team was gearing up. I saw Judgmental Mom standing by the popcorn machine.

"Hi!" I said, walking up to her. "You look busy!"

She half-smiled and nodded but didn't meet my eyes.

"Alexis, why don't you help make popcorn?" I said.

"Great idea!" Alexis replied cheerily, picking up some empty bags to fill.

Judgmental Mom's body visibly tensed, but she didn't say anything. My daughter looked at me knowingly and grinned.

They filled bags together for about ten minutes. With that finished, Judgmental Mom walked away and started setting up the canteen.

"What should I do now?" Alexis called over to me.

"The canteen always gets busy. Why don't you help out with that?"

"Okay," she said and walked over. Judgmental Mom looked defeated.

For the next two hours, they worked side by side at the busiest station. The canteen requires a lot of communication to run smoothly. In other words, Judgmental Mom had to talk to my kid. She wasn't chatty with Alexis, but she wasn't unfriendly either.

I sat at the ticket booth nearby and waited. Eventually, I heard what I wanted to hear: "Alexis, can you hand that girl a water bottle?"

Bingo. You just used my daughter's chosen name, Judgmental Mom. I bet Jesus would be proud.

———

Exposure is important. If you haven't experienced something personally and learned about it that way, the next best thing is to learn from someone who has. The problem is, a lot of folks have no exposure to trans people in their day-to-day lives, at least that they know of.

That's the key thing here: *that they know of*. It's hard to pinpoint exactly what percentage of the population is trans, but it's probably safe to say that we've all met at least a few trans people. Perhaps we don't know they're trans because they haven't told us—they may not even be out to themselves yet—but that doesn't make them less so. Just like someone doesn't "turn gay," they don't "turn trans." It's a part of a person from birth.

My guess was that Judgmental Mom had never met a person she knew was trans. That, coupled with a religious upbringing steeped in outdated ideas about the LGBTQ community, led her to form opinions of trans people that were based on fear, not facts. In this way, I could relate to her. I had chastised the choices made by the parents raising their gender-neutral baby for similar reasons. I thought I knew better based on the facts I had—but I didn't have *all the facts*. That's why Alexis and I had decided to give Judgmental Mom some facts upon which to build new opinions. And to do it in the nicest way possible.

Alexis had always been a sweet kid, but we were now seeing

more of her personality come through. She was fun to hang out with, precocious and hilarious, making great conversation with kids and adults alike. We gently corralled Judgmental Mom into having contact with her whenever we could. Alexis spent several events working alongside her. Eventually, Judgmental Mom relaxed a little. They became chatty and I think she might have almost forgotten she disapproved of Alexis's "lifestyle."

I don't know if I believe that people are put in your path for a reason, but I do know that woman taught our family a few lessons. Alexis learned she should enter any space as if she belonged there, regardless of how people treated her. She learned to expect respect, even if others aren't willing to give it easily. As someone who would likely face discrimination throughout her life, she needed this critical lesson. I wanted her to know that her worth comes from within, and not from how others might value her. It had taken me decades to internalize that one.

For my part, I learned how to be more assertive. I stopped letting Judgmental Mom ignore me and made myself a part of her conversations. When she approached a group of us and talked only to the other people there, I would address her directly, sometimes complimenting her on her outfit or crouching down to joke around with her kids. I made it so she couldn't ignore me without looking like a garbage person—and who wants to look like a garbage person?

My family belonged too. We were worthy of respect too.

Eventually, Judgmental Mom and her family left the school for another, and I learned through mutual acquaintances that she had never really changed her mind about us. She still thought we were lousy parents to a confused child. I guess there's a lesson even in that: people don't change overnight. Judgmental Mom may need to be exposed to a few more trans people and their families to realize how wrong she is on this one. Or maybe she'll never learn.

But we tried. And once again, as I had with Sylvia, I was able to show one of my children how to lead with love—even if that's not what you're getting back.

fallout

EARLY ON IN ALEXIS'S TRANSITION, I was left with another concern that kept me up at night. During recent years, my blog, *The Maven of Mayhem*, had become more than a website where I anonymously ranted about the life of mediocre motherhood. The audience had grown to include people across Canada and the US. It wasn't a high-traffic site, but it had enough of a readership that I was sometimes asked to appear at local events and was occasionally stopped on the street by someone who recognized me.

I was no longer writing semi-anonymously either. There was a picture of me and a few old ones of the kids on the site. Some people jokingly called me "Maven" when they met me, but everyone knew my name.

My blog was my fourth baby. I loved writing it and sharing it with people. I mostly kept to lighter topics, but sometimes touched on heavier material. I made no money off the site, other than when an editor occasionally reached out after reading a piece and offered me work. In that way, it was a great showcase of what I could do, but I had no paid content, no giveaways and no product reviews. It was all personal essays. As a freelance writer and editor, I wanted one spot on the internet that was entirely mine, and themavenofmayhem.com was it.

But now I was considering shutting it down.

My family had always figured prominently in my posts, particularly my three boys. As it turned out, I didn't have three boys. How would I explain that? *Should* I explain it? I feared it would put my daughter at risk to out her online.

After much thought, I decided to shut it down quietly and take my existing social media pages offline. I could create new business accounts and a new site exclusively to sell my content. But no more personal essays. My career was writing, but my most important job was to protect my children.

"You can't do that!" Alexis said when I announced the plan at the dinner table the following night. "Mom, it's your *blog*! You love your blog."

"No," I said. "I *love* you. I *like* my blog. I can live without my blog. I can't live without you."

"Why do you have to shut it down?" Jackson asked.

"Because I'm worried that if I tell everyone about your sister, they might be mean to her."

"So you don't want people to know about her?" he asked, trying to figure it out.

"No, that's not it," I said. "I just want Alexis to have the choice to tell people or not tell them."

"Do you know how awkward this is going to be?" Alexis said. "In a few months, when I look like I want to look, people who used to read your blog all the time are going to see us on the street and wonder when you got a daughter and what happened to your other son."

"Awwwkwaaard," said Jackson, making a face.

" If you just say it, everyone will know," she explained. "You just have to do it once instead of over and over. That's easier."

" She has a point," Aerik piped up. "A lot of people in Ottawa know you, Mom. How many times do you want to have the same conversation?"

This was not exactly how I'd expected this talk to go.

" Maybe you could use it as an advocacy platform," my partner offered. "You don't use the kids' names on there anyway, do you?" I didn't. I had given them nicknames, or handles: Aerik was Intrepid, Jackson was Spawnling and Alexis was Gutsy—which, come to think of it, was rather fitting. I also had no recent pictures of the kids on the site. Nobody would know what Alexis looked like.

"You should do that!" Alexis agreed. "When I searched for trans kids in Canada, I couldn't find any stories of families who were supportive. Not one. We should be that one."

We should be that one.

—

My kids have grown up online, where people share a lot of themselves in exchange for clicks, likes and upvotes. Everyone wants to be a YouTube celebrity. Everyone wants to be the next star. But I was worried that they didn't understand the permanency of it all. Privacy is not a genie you can put back in the bottle. Deleting something does not necessarily make it go away. Did they know about caches? Or that screenshots can haunt you forever?

And what about hate groups? Some have entire databases on LGBTQ advocates, where they collect as much information as possible to use against them. People have had their phone numbers, workplaces, home addresses and credit card numbers shared publicly, simply for daring to speak out. It's a practice called doxxing, and it happens far more than many realize.

That was one side of the equation, and it was an important one. But the other side was also important.

Somewhere, there was a kid searching for stories of other kids who came out and were still loved. Somewhere else, there were worried parents looking for examples of affirming families so they could have something to model. And somewhere else, there were parents who refused to support their trans child because everyone around them said it was just a phase and the kid would grow out it. How did they know? Because when they went searching for answers online, that's what they found first.

It's not as if there weren't positive examples out there—there were even a handful in Canada. But they were hard to find, which is why Alexis had been unsuccessful. Putting another positive example out there could help tip the scales; it could even become the first thing people see when they go looking for answers.

The world was scary for trans people, and especially for trans kids. But it was scary only because the narrative was still predominantly negative. The only way to make it safer was to change that narrative, to get people thinking about trans people in a positive light. And to do that, people had to offer positive examples.

Yes, it was a risk—a big one. But the more conversations we had, the more I realized it was one our family was willing to take.

Alexis came out to the world in several steps. Family, close friends and the people at school were all told quickly. I then created a Facebook list with the names of trusted people and shared the news with them. So far, so good. We stayed in that space for a little while, with only the near and dear in the know, enjoying the relative comfort and safety. But we knew it couldn't last. Eventually, everyone in our lives needed to be told. Families go about this in different ways. Some tell people individually and some get groups together. Others take the social media or email approach, giving their loved ones space to fully absorb the news and get over any initial shock before they speak in person. There are families who don't make a sweeping declaration at all, but instead let it happen organically, one person and one encounter at a time. And sadly, there are still those who live in areas where the threat of being out is so high that they tell no one at all. Those families sometimes move to a different city or another part of the country, where their child can live as their true gender without anyone knowing they're trans. There's nothing wrong with that, of course. But it should be a personal decision, not one based in fear of intolerance or worse.

In our case, the big coming-out-to-the-rest-of-the-world happened on my blog. I spent hours writing and rewriting a post. When it came time to pick a title, I chose "My Son Has Changed. My Love Hasn't" and added a photo of pink high-tops. In the post, I told the world that the person I had thought was my son was in fact my daughter, and that we loved her no matter what. I asked people to be kind, urging them to please step out of our lives quietly if they weren't going to be supportive.

"I am writing this post because it gives you time to decide if you can accept my child on her terms," I explained near the end. "If you can see her for more than her gender; if you can understand how important this is to her. If you can't do this, please exit our lives, stage left. I won't be mad, just relieved that we didn't have to have a big ugly confrontation about it. See, we can only have people in our lives that support her. I'm not trying to be a jerk, just a mom. Kid trumps unsupportive friend or family member. I hope you understand."

Reading the post now makes me wince a little. It's riddled with problematic language like "transgendered." People aren't "gayed" and they're also not "transgendered." Transgender isn't something that happens to you—it's something you are. But you know, coming from someone who was still quite new to this, it's not the worst post out there. The point is clear: our child is trans, we're still learning, she comes first, please use the right pronouns and don't be unkind.

I remember I pressed Publish and then had an epic anxiety attack. The genie was now out, and so were we.

The first few minutes after I shared the blog post were absolute hell. I was afraid of what the response would be. I was also afraid that people would not respond. What would be worse? I couldn't decide.

Before long, I was getting stacks of notifications on my phone. I could see that the post was being commented on, but I couldn't see what the comments were from my lock screen. Were they supportive or ugly? Were we headed toward a welcoming love-glitter rainbow, or off a precipice into Tea Party-topia? Someone without a timeshare at Anxiety Villa might have walked away for a few hours, or maybe even gone to bed and checked in on things over a bagel in the a.m. After all, it's not like I could do much, right? The news was out there, and whatever happened was going to happen whether I watched it unfold live or not.

Sadly, I have a swanky condo at Anxiety Villa and I visit regularly. There was no way I could sleep, so I paced the proverbial penthouse as I opened my social media apps and had a look.

There were piles of messages waiting for us from loved ones and strangers alike: comments, tweets, emails, PMs. And nearly every one felt like a hug.

We support your child in being the best version of herself.
Your daughter is so brave.
I love your family.
Thank you for doing the right thing.
I wish there were more people like you.
If she needs anything, I'm here for her.
You're amazing parents.
We're so happy for Gutsy!

Gutsy. I'm glad she had that name. It made it all feel safer somehow, like I was protecting her anonymity while also sharing our story. It was the best of both worlds. I couldn't wait to tell Alexis and the rest of the family we had struck gold in the community support department.

I noticed the next morning that my Facebook friends list had dropped by a few people. My attention was fully on Alexis as I tried to shield her from any potential hate thrown her way. But I did notice, and I wondered who had decided to exit our lives. There were also some notable absences from the list of people expressing their support. A few friends who had been in our lives for many years and regularly read and commented on my blog had said nothing in response to my now-viral post. They continued to say nothing in the days that followed.

I waited. And I hurt.

Of all the people in my life, there were some I'd expected to hop on board the support train right away—close friends whose kids were growing up with mine, had gone to playgroup or school with us and had come to all the birthday parties. I had supported several of them through tough times in their lives, from miscarriages to worrisome diagnoses. Yet they were nowhere to be seen when I needed them. They hadn't completely jumped ship; they were still on my friends list, but they weren't behaving like friends.

And I really needed my friends right then.

For the record, if someone needs more time to process important new information, that's understandable. But there's a great way to communicate that to the sender. That person can say something like this:

> Hi, Person I Care About,
> I just want to let you know that I saw your news about X. This is very new to me and I need some time to learn about it. But I want you to know I'm thinking of you and am not ignoring you. I'll be in touch soon.

Of course, that's in an ideal situation, where emotions haven't taken over completely. Real life is messier, and we don't always behave in ideal ways. (I've been guilty of that so many times that I could write a whole other book about it.)

Some people fell out of our life without saying a word. I thought rejection would hurt less as an adult. But given that this rejection seemed directly related to the core of who my child is, it hurt even more. I hurt for me, but I especially hurt for her. Who had she harmed? What had she done to deserve this?

One friend did not slink away quietly, but instead spoke up quite loudly—and when she did, I immediately wished she hadn't. Her words were like a punch to the gut, her judgment harsh. She insisted on calling Alexis by her old name and using male pronouns, even though I'd asked her not to. She did it publicly and deliberately. Raw from the exchange and feeling highly defensive of my child, I told her where to go. I had no energy to give to people who refused to show compassion to a struggling child and her family.

In other circumstances, I might have reached out to those people. But I didn't because I couldn't. I was exhausted and teetering on depression. This big change, which felt like a crisis at the time, had drained my emotional gas tank. I was running on fumes and didn't have a drop to give to friends who were struggling with the news in their own ways. Their job, I believed, was to be there for me and my family as I had been there for them at other times.

The human brain is hard-wired to prioritize negative experiences. When we get close to a fire, it will remind us of the one time we burned ourselves on something hot before it reminds us of all those times we safely and happily roasted marshmallows. It's a protective measure, and a good one. Learning and evolution at work.

In this case, however, my brain's primitive priority filtering didn't work in my favour. Logically, I knew from the reaction on social media, the texts and phone calls, and the in-person visits from loved ones who just wanted to hug Alexis or bring her a little coming-out gift that we had an impressive support system. Go, team! Yet my mind wandered most often to the people who were gone, not the ones who were still there. I felt those losses deeply. Sometimes, I still do.

Rejection always reminds me that I'm still that kid in the schoolyard wondering why no one will play with her. I'm still the young girl with her legs swinging on the stool, finding out that her father left before he could get to know her.

Except now I had a daughter, and she was being rejected too.

And we weren't the only ones dealing with the fallout. My mom had a long-time friend in her neighbourhood. They had raised children together, gone through crises together and spoke nearly every day by phone. When my mom wasn't home, I knew there were three places she'd likely be, and that friend's house was one of them. She was like an aunt to me.

For weeks after Alexis came out, my mom's phone remained silent. Her friend did not reach out. My mom had a sneaking suspicion there was an issue and readied herself for it as best she could. When they finally did speak, the friend made it clear she disapproved of, and would not accept, Alexis's transition.

"Well," my mom said sadly, "then you don't leave me with any choice, I'm afraid. If it comes down to you or my granddaughter, there's no competition."

My mom lost a lifelong friendship that day. She will tell you it hurt, but it was a simple decision to make. Family is her top priority.

Love always comes first.

Meanwhile, my sister, Katie, was getting married. The date had been announced several weeks before Alexis came out. At the time, Katie had asked Aerik and Alexis to be ushers. I was one of her bridesmaids.

"Alexis, I just want to make sure you're still comfortable being part of the wedding party," Katie said.

"I am," said Alexis, "as long as I can be me when I'm doing it."

"Of course!" her aunt replied. "You can wear whatever feels good. I want you to be comfortable."

Katie meant it. My sister had been planning her wedding since she was old enough to know what weddings were. Despite knowing exactly how she wanted the day to look, she gave Alexis free rein to choose her own style and came shopping with us to cheer her on and tell her how beautiful she looked.

The programs had been printed a while back with Alexis's old name on them. Without the slightest hesitation, Katie and her fiancé, Rob, ordered new ones.

But there was one problem: our mother's lifelong friend had been invited to the wedding but was now adamantly opposed to Alexis's transition. After some discussion with my mom, they decided she would be uninvited—not to be spiteful, but to ensure Alexis was surrounded by people who would make her first big public appearance as herself as positive as possible.

The night before the wedding, Katie invited her bridesmaids and her only female usher to the bridal suite for a sleepover. She wanted Alexis to take part in all the excitement. In the morning, the bridesmaids helped Alexis with her makeup and hair. She glowed, both inside and out.

I have several pictures of my daughter that day, smiling proudly in black dress pants and a bright pink blouse that matched the bridesmaid dresses. On top of pulling off a gorgeous ceremony, Katie achieved her goal of making her niece feel comfortable and accepted.

When negativity sees itself out, all that's left is positivity. Alexis was surrounded by it all day.

ELEVEN

affirmation

ONCE ALEXIS HAD TOLD US she wasn't a boy, one of the most pressing issues was to ensure that she didn't keep developing in the wrong direction. We needed to stop her puberty.

Of all the issues facing trans kids, by far the most controversial are the medical treatments. Those who oppose medical support prior to adulthood, such as puberty blockers and hormone replacement therapy, argue that it causes irreparable damage to children. I would argue the opposite: that failing to provide medical support when needed can put young lives at risk. This stance is supported by recent reliable studies tracking trans youth, as well as the world's leading pediatric medical organizations.

The trans community has one of the highest rates of suicide of any marginalized group. There are many reasons for this, but most can be boiled down to one truth: society treats trans people terribly. A big part of that awfulness is a refusal to believe trans people are who they say they are. Imagine for a minute having to fight every day of your life to be seen as yourself. Imagine having to prove or justify your gender to loved ones, co-workers, neighbours, medical staff and potential romantic partners. Imagine being misgendered all the time. Imagine being called "miss" five times a day when you're not a woman. Imagine being told you're mentally ill simply for living as yourself. Imagine seeing hate groups lobby governments to deny you basic human rights. Imagine being questioned, doubted, ridiculed, belittled and told repeatedly that others know you better than you know yourself.

Being trans isn't what causes the high rates of self-harm; it's the cisgender people—those of us who identify with the gender we were assigned at birth—who do. And one of our biggest targets is also the most vulnerable: trans kids.

People love to question the very existence of trans youth. They like to say that these kids are too young to know their gender, that they're simply confused, and that parents and medical professionals, brainwashed by trans activists, are guiding them down a dangerous and irreversible path. As proof, they cite largely debunked studies showing a "desistance" rate of over 80 percent. They claim the bulk of young patients at a gender identity clinic went on to live as the gender they were assigned at birth. They call affirming parents child abusers. (I've lost count of how many times that insult has been hurled my way.) They protest school boards that include trans education in the curriculum or allow young people to use the bathroom that matches their identity. They attack doctors who provide treatment for trans children.

These people harm trans kids and are on the wrong side of history. They may think they're right, but they're not. How could they be? It's like a white person telling a person of colour there's no such thing as racism. Despite having no lived experience, they still believe they know better than the people who are dealing with it first-hand. That's not only foolish but also dangerous.

So when it came to the question of medical support, we chose to listen to our child rather than the opinions of people who are not transgender. What did she need? What could we help with? We reached out to the trans community to find out how we could do this right, and we sought help from the Children's Hospital of Eastern Ontario, whose medical experts had been working with gender-diverse youth for several years.

Alexis will tell you that our assistance saved her life. Statisticians would agree. Research has found that when trans children are given strong support by their parents, their rate of attempted suicide drops to nearly that of the average cisgender child. Again, being trans is not the problem—a lack of support is.

I had put Alexis on the list for the hospital's gender diversity clinic the week after she came out because I knew it could take a while to get her in. I suspected she was in the very early stages of puberty at that point. At the first appointment a few weeks later, my spouse and I met with the social worker, a friendly young guy with a great smile who also co-facilitated the support group we had been attending. This was a meeting to go over the basics, which, we all realized, we already knew.

The next couple of appointments were with one of the doctors. To receive medical treatment at the clinic, patients had to meet the criteria for gender dysphoria, a feeling of deep discomfort or distress about living as the gender assigned at birth. Not all trans people experience this, but many who do require medical intervention to ease that distress.

The studies showing large desistance rates often conflate gender identity and gender expression. The difference is important. Gender identity is how you identify: man, woman, non-binary (a term used by many people who don't fit neatly into the gender binary concept of "man" or "woman") or something else entirely. Gender expression is how you express who you are on the outside: your mannerisms, your clothes, your hairstyle. A boy who likes to wear dresses but still identifies as a boy is not trans-gender. Some of these studies mix this all up and package it as one finding, but it's apples and oranges. And neither gender identity nor gender expression is in any way related to a person's sexual orientation. Trans people can be gay, straight, bisexual, pansexual or asexual, just like the rest of the population.

Furthermore, one of the desistance studies measured gender identity by who kept returning to the clinic for treatment. When the researchers found that many kids stopped coming, they concluded it was because those kids weren't trans. But maybe they felt uncomfortable there. Maybe they found treatment elsewhere. Maybe some of them felt it was too unsafe to be themselves and went back into the closet. Maybe their parents refused to help them transition. And yes, maybe some of them truly weren't trans. But I don't think leaving a clinic is a reliable scientific indicator of someone's gender identity.

Trans children and their parents are constantly under attack because of incomplete or biased studies like these. Thankfully, there are more current and reliable studies that show largely positive outcomes for young people who are affirmed at home, in the community and by the medical professionals who work with them. They have significantly lower rates of depression and suicide, along with higher rates of happiness.

But we didn't need those studies to know what to do. We just needed to listen to what our child was telling us.

—

Within a few sessions, Alexis was diagnosed with gender dysphoria. The doctor was impressed by how self-aware she was and how well she could describe her feelings. That diagnosis opened the door for her to receive medical care that would change her life for the better.

For trans kids, natal puberty can be traumatic and can also cause a lifetime of pain. In the case of a girl with testosterone driving the body bus, puberty can trigger changes to height, skeletal structure, facial features, hair growth and voice that are either impossible or difficult and costly to undo. Many trans people who went through puberty prior to transitioning have spent tens of thousands of dollars trying to undo what hormones did to them in their teen years—that is, if they can afford it. Most of these treatments are not covered by public or private health insurance. They're considered cosmetic procedures.

Of course, not all trans and non-binary people need or want medical support. Some are comfortable with their bodies just the way they are. But for many I talked to, puberty caused distress, and much of what can be changed is unaffordable.

"If you can do one thing for your daughter," a new trans friend told me, "get her on puberty blockers as soon as she needs them. It will save her a lot of pain, trust me." I had no idea puberty blockers existed, and I wondered what the side effects of halting hormone production could be.

We didn't have to wait long to find out. Alexis's first appointment with the CHEO endocrinologist specializing in trans youth involved a long chat, her own assessment of Alexis's dysphoria and a blood test. The doctor was kind and smart, and she treated Alexis like a partner in her own medical journey. I liked her immediately. She explained that there are five stages of puberty, and that it's ideal to stop it in stage two, in part for better surgical outcomes in adulthood.

I was fascinated. Now I knew that there were puberty blockers and stages of puberty, and that doctors had really thought this out for long-term success. Not all trans people want surgeries, but it's good to have those options.

"What happens if she changes her mind and doesn't want the blockers anymore?" I asked privately. As far as I had come in the last little while, there was still a part of me that struggled with the idea of doing anything permanent.

"Then we stop them," the doctor said. "All blockers do is hit the pause button. They give kids a while to figure out where they want to go. If we take her off them, the body kicks back into gear and puberty continues."

That seemed like a reasonable first step to me. But most importantly, it was a critical one for Alexis, who had been saying she needed this to happen as soon as possible. Her body, her choice.

We got a call a few days later. "Alex is in stage three," the nurse explained.

"Wow," I said. "I wasn't expecting that."

"We could tell right away she was at stage two or three," she said. "But we've seen a lot of puberty here."

Testosterone is sneaky. Unlike estrogen, it can initiate early changes with next to no fanfare. That's why cisgender girls tend to develop faster than boys for a year or two, before the boys catch up. Estrogen is quick, then slows down. Testosterone is slow, then speeds up.

We had caught it in the nick of time.

—

I was now getting daily emails and Facebook messages from people around the world who were reading my blog. Several told me they were being investigated by local child protection services simply for raising their trans children in an affirming way. One person from a small town in South America said they could never transition because not only would their family disown them but they would be in real danger of being assaulted or murdered. A US parent said her teen was on suicide watch because the family had no insurance and couldn't afford the $1,200 a month for a blocker, let alone any hormones.

In Ontario, the only thing we had to pay for was the hormone blocker. I was floored when I saw the bill for that, though. A single monthly injection was around $450. We were fortunate to have private drug insurance through my partner's work that covered 80 percent. Later, we were able to bump it up to 100 percent.

Telling our story had allowed us to see what life was like for other families with transgender kids, which was sobering. Our daughter's ride, overall, had been smoother than most. But it wasn't without its bumps.

A few weeks after Alexis had come out to us, I noticed her starting to slip into a darker place again. She was withdrawing to her room more often and resisting going to school. She had come a long way since that terrible night she spent cowering under the covers. Now it felt like she was regressing.

"What's up? You haven't been yourself lately," I asked. "You seemed happier for a while, but not so much right now."

She sighed and looked out the window. "It's the kids in my class. A lot of them don't get it."

"Don't get being trans?"

"Yeah. They don't understand."

She had been gung-ho about coming out at school in the beginning—backed by a teacher and two classmates she had confided in early on—but she had quickly put the brakes on. She was growing her hair and had started wearing clothes exclusively from the girls' department, but nothing that screamed pink-glitter-explosion femininity; she was subtle about it. After hesitating for a while, she had asked her classmates to call her Alex, and to use the pronouns "she" and "her." But most of the students in her class had not received any education in transgender issues. They didn't understand why this kid was changing names and pronouns.

Alexis tried to quash misconceptions with facts. "I told them what transgender means and I thought that would help," she said. "It didn't make it better."

At this point, the kids split into two groups: those who mocked her and those who avoided her. A group of three boys she knew well now called her "tranny" and "faggot" whenever the opportunity arose. The rest of her classmates, not knowing how to adapt to the change, pretended she wasn't there. When she walked up to them, they walked away. When she spoke, they ignored her.

"What about your friends? Those girls you confided in?" I asked.

"Mom, they're grade six girls. They don't want to be seen with me because they'll get made fun of too. They joined the Avoiding Alexis Club."

I felt my heart breaking into pieces. My daughter had been brave enough to tell the world who she really was, and now she was all alone with that truth every day. I remembered what it felt like to be alone. This was ten times worse, though, because it was my child going through it instead of me.

She started to cry. "I can't do this," she said.

I held her close, holding in my own tears. "Oh, honey," I said. "We're going to make this better, I promise."

———

The Ten Oaks Project is a camp in Ontario that caters specifically to LGBTQ youth and the children of queer parents (lovingly known as "queerlings" or "queerspawn"). For a few magical days, these kids and teens get to be in an environment where they don't have to hide their identities or continually explain themselves and their families to others. It's a haven for youth who don't necessarily have that anywhere else.

Alexis was keen to go. The only issue was a serious lack of funds. The camp cost hundreds of dollars, which we simply didn't have. We were a family of five living on mostly one income. My work was very part time, as I was spending much of my time trying to finish high school through online courses. Ten Oaks does provide subsidies for families in need, but we didn't feel "in need" enough to take that subsidy from someone who could use it more.

A friend strongly suggested we set up a GoFundMe campaign, an idea that made me hugely uncomfortable. Again, we weren't struggling to eat—we just didn't have money for extras. There's a difference, and having been hungry before, I recognized it.

"If you don't do it, someone else will do it for you," she said. I think she was talking about herself. That would have felt even weirder. *Fine.* I sucked it up for my daughter's sake.

The GoFundMe went live around 10 p.m. on a weekday evening in mid-June. I had created a fundraiser called "Let's Get Gutsy to Camp!" and set a goal. On the campaign page, I admitted how weird this was for me, but I said that I'd rather be uncomfortable than see my daughter disappointed. I shared the link on social media and figured that even if we raised only a few hundred dollars, it would make a solid dent.

Twelve hours later, the internet had raised all of Alexis's camp money plus an extra $300 to subsidize another camper's trip. It came from friends, family, blog readers and even complete strangers who had seen the link and wanted to help. I couldn't believe it. People just wanted my awesome kid to have an awesome time at an awesome camp. Alexis was an overjoyed tween when I told her she was going. And that summer, she not only made some great friends but also came home with a new confidence and a strong sense of self.

Thanks, internet.

It was good that Alexis had an affirming camp to look forward to, because there were ongoing issues at school that were anything but affirming to a trans child.

One day, I got an email informing me that the school was conducting a sexual and health education class, and that I might want to consider keeping Alexis home that day. They were separating boys and girls, as is often the case. The boys would be learning about testosterone-driven puberty and wet dreams.

The girls would be learning about estrogen-driven puberty, including menstruation. These lessons were geared exclusively to kids who are cisgender and didn't take into consideration those who are not.

"I don't fit into either of those boxes right now," Alexis said. "I'm not a boy, so I don't belong in that session. I'm a girl, but I'm never going to get a period or anything. Besides, the other girls might not like me being there."

In other words, the girls didn't see her as a fellow girl, which made me sad. If there had been better LGBTQ education in the classroom, students would have learned that not all girls are born with the same body parts, and it wouldn't have been a problem for my daughter to deal with.

At the time, that type of education was in the pipeline in Ontario. The then Liberal government had announced more comprehensive health education in all schools, which was to include learning about trans issues at the elementary level. Some parents were in an uproar, with news outlets covering petitions and protests. But many parents of LGBTQ kids were excited. We were coping with what happens when children don't get that education. Our kids were being bullied and ostracized, and some were taking their lives because of it. In the short time since Alexis came out, I had already spoken to parents whose children were dead because they felt they would never be accepted by their peers.

Meanwhile, conservative politicians and pastors were screaming about innocence lost and confusing young minds with information they didn't need to hear. "This type of thing doesn't belong in schools!" people would (and still do) cry out. "They can be taught this at home!" But taught by whom, exactly? Parents who hadn't received the education themselves? Who might offer kids sketchy facts tainted by their own biases? And what about those who decide not to tell their kids anything at all? I believe acceptance begins at home, but not all households are at the same starting point. In some homes, there are educational, religious and cultural barriers that make tolerance more challenging. Hell, even in our liberal, atheist household, I had been grossly ignorant about what it meant to be transgender and the issues facing that population.

Like it or not, LGBTQ people exist in the world, in all walks of life, and all our kids will be interacting with them. More importantly, some of our children are a part of that community too, whether they're aware of it yet or not. Educating *everyone* means all our children grow up in a safer and more accepting world. We can foster inclusion at home, but if we don't also foster it in the public education system, we're not a truly inclusive society.

In Ontario in 2014, health and sexual education classes were still predominantly geared toward straight cisgender kids. People who didn't fit the mould would not see themselves represented. We could have insisted that Alexis attend, as it was her right to do so. She could not be discriminated against on the grounds of gender identity. However, we decided to conserve our energy for things that really mattered to her. This wasn't one of them.

One thing that did matter to her was the end-of-year trip. The grade six classes had been fundraising for most of the year to pay for a day of sports and activities at a local university. A few weeks before the big day, I got an email from the teacher and sighed in frustration. There were no gender-neutral washrooms available to the students, the teacher said, and everyone would be using gendered group change rooms. I knew that was not going to work for Alexis. It was too early in her transition for her to be comfortable. After fundraising for most of the year, she was going to miss the big school trip.

The news sunk her morale even further. Alexis was already refusing to get out of bed most days, her attendance was poor, she had no friends, and now she couldn't fully participate in the curriculum or go on the field trip. I hadn't seen her that low in a long time. The staff noticed it too. She was shutting down at school, not completing her work or engaging in class discussions. "I'm worried we're losing her," one of the staff members said with tears in her eyes.

Being trans was not the problem for Alexis. The problem was how society treated her.

In early June, we pulled Alexis out of school. We could have waited until the year was finished, but there was no point. She couldn't go on the school trip and she feared she'd be ridiculed for wearing a dress at her grade six graduation. Alexis knew who she was, but the world wasn't seeing her that way yet. She had just begun to take hormone blockers and was waiting for them to start working. Meanwhile, she was dealing with the full impact of dys-phoria. She hated her body; she didn't want to care for it, look at it or acknowledge it for what it was. It would sometimes take several hours of encouragement before she'd bathe, and then I'd hear her sobbing in the shower. Then I would cry too.

We had to do something or risk losing her.

Alexis and I decided she wouldn't go to middle school. Instead, I would homeschool her while doing my own online classes. That way, she could go through early transition and rejoin her classmates in high school. We hoped they would have matured by then, and Alexis would have two years to transition in relative safety.

TWELVE

mainstream

IN THE FALL OF 2014, I won the award for worst teacher. I don't know how many people were competing for this prestigious prize, but it doesn't matter because I deserved it. I don't know what's wrong with me. For a person who loves kids, I'm embarrassingly bad at kid-centred careers. Daycare wasn't my forte, I was only passable as a teacher's assistant, and I was a complete embarrassment at teaching middle-school math.

Alexis and I did our best that year to keep up with the curriculum—and failed miserably. We did, however, read *To Kill a Mockingbird*, which I consider a rousing success. It's my favourite book, and to read it with my daughter and see her fall in love with the story made the whole year worthwhile. She immediately grasped several of the deeper concepts in the book—themes that had taken me a few high school essays to fully wrap my head around. Once again, I was a proud mom.

I didn't lean on her too hard to learn algebra or the periodic table. More than anything, I wanted her to catch her breath after years of internal torment. The 2014–15 school year was all about self-discovery. It was a solid decision. Her confidence grew, along with her hair, which was a rich medium brown, full and shiny. Slowly, we started to see her smile more often—and not the shy smiles she used to give, but big, happy grins. We would hear her laugh and wonder aloud how long it had been since she found so much joy around her.

We were on our way to an appointment one afternoon when Alexis asked if we could get something to drink.

"I'll never say no to coffee," I replied and pulled into the Starbucks drive-through.

When the barista handed us our drinks, she said, "Have a great day, ladies!"

Alexis beamed.

"She called us ladies! So cool," my daughter said, leaning back in her seat and sipping her drink triumphantly.

It was the first time she had been acknowledged as a girl by someone who didn't know her. My heart beat excitedly, and it wasn't just because of the caffeine.

One day in the early spring of 2015, I received an email from a CBC reporter. She had been reading my blog and wanted to do a story on our family for local radio.

I had entered a comfortable space blogging about raising a trans child. I confined my pictures of Alexis to my personal Facebook profile and had asked others to do the same. I was still using the name Gutsy when referring to her in any public online setting. With the blog, I was doing what my family and I felt was important without sacrificing certain elements of our privacy. It was a good balance.

I had recently written about Alexis in a local magazine about supporting trans kids in Ottawa. But I'd made sure the photos I took of her didn't show her face. Instead, I went for the artistic approach, photographing her from the neck down or getting a close-up of her fun multicoloured shoes. It added a personal touch while maintaining her anonymity.

An interview with CBC Radio would throw a wrench into the works. I knew if we did this, our names and photos would appear in the accompanying written piece on the CBC website. Once out there, the genie could not be put back into the bottle. I tensed at the thought. Alexis was a twelve-year-old trans kid in a world that wasn't quite ready for her yet.

When I called the journalist, Hallie Cotnam, she said she had never done a piece like this, but wanted to do it justice. I could hear the sincerity in her voice. She truly hoped to introduce her listeners to something new and positive. I promised her an answer soon.

After a healthy family discussion and an impressive anxiety attack on my part, we decided to do the interview. We hoped our story would help Canadians understand transgender kids. We knew the risks, but the potential rewards far outweighed them.

Hallie arrived one weekday morning and the whole family participated, describing events from the email Alexis sent us on the eve of Pink Shirt Day to my decision to blog about her transition. I looked around the living room and smiled. My family, for its flaws, was full of love. I listened as Aerik and Jackson talked about how brave their sister was, and I teared up as my spouse compellingly answered questions from "a dad's point of view." But Alexis, once a little wallflower, stole the show. It was her moment to tell the world who she was and make them see why they should accept her. She killed it. She was sweet, well spoken and so relatable. She was proof that once you get to know trans children on a personal level, you realize that they're just regular kids who happen to be trans. That was what we wanted to get across.

Hallie contacted me a couple of days later to say that the piece would air the following morning. This was it.

I sat quietly for a minute, collecting my thoughts. Was there anything I should do before tomorrow? Yes, there was. My blog readers had been following our family's journey through transition for over a year. It only felt right to introduce them to Alexis before CBC Radio aired the interview. I went online and wrote the post that would change how I talked about my family forever, entitling it "World, Meet My Daughter."

"Okay. Deep Breath." I began. "This is about to be the second-hardest post I've written on this blog. I'm not the best at handling change."

I recounted how my family had opened our doors to journalists. "What this means is that very soon, the world—or at least our corner of it—will know our daughter's real name and what she looks like," I wrote. "It's big, scary stuff."

I went on to explain why we had chosen to do this. "We know it's a decision that carries risk, but we also know it can carry a lot of hope." I followed up that statement with a picture of Alexis, one bright blue eye visible under brown bangs with hot-pink streaks. It was my favourite photo of her, taken first thing in the morning, as she was about to get out bed. A natural beauty illuminated her face.

"Here we are," I wrote in closing. "We're *out* out. I won't lie and tell you I'm not afraid. Of course I am. But Alexis is choosing to step up and make the world a better place, and that fills me with far more hope than fear. So no matter what happens in the next little while, I know we chose hope over fear. And that means hope wins."

I hit the Publish button before I could think about it too hard. Now the regulars who read my blog would see Alexis before she made it onto the CBC website. I went on about my day.

While I was at the grocery store, a friend texted me. "Your daughter's face is everywhere!" she wrote.

I shot back my own text: "What do you mean?"

"EVERYWHERE!" came the reply in all caps. "Alex is blowing up the internet."

I checked Facebook.

Yes, she was everywhere. "World, Meet My Daughter" was being shared and retweeted constantly. It was madness. My feed filled up with tag notifications and pictures of my daughter's beautiful face, her pink-streaked hair falling over one eye. We heard not only from friends but also from some of her old teachers, former neighbours and colleagues, and a host of complete strangers. Thankfully, nearly every comment on the three platforms where it was shared—my blog, Facebook and Twitter—was positive. So much love for one brave little girl.

Alexis's name and face were now part of a bigger movement: the affirmation of transgender children. It was 2015 and the scales were starting to tip.

The CBC story aired the following morning. We nervously listened in while making school lunches in the kitchen. Hallie had a knack for taking the best ten minutes of a two-hour interview and turning them into something memorable. It was a warm, compassionate piece on supporting our child and what that meant to all of us. It was one of two CBC features on our family to win an award.

A couple of hours later, I got a call from a reporter with the TV news division of the network. The listener response to our family's story had been so positive that he wanted to talk to us for the evening news. Could he come right now? Alexis shrugged when I asked her. Why not? We were already that day's talk of the town.

"Okay, but the house is gross," I said. The journalist laughed and assured me they were used to filming around mess. That did not stop me from rigorously cleaning (and swearing under my breath while I did it).

By 11 a.m., we had a news truck in our driveway and a camera in our faces. The journalist was kind, but we did have to correct some of the language and ideas he used. For example, we corrected the notion that Alexis was "born a boy." She wasn't. She was always a girl, but she was assigned male at birth based on her body's appearance. The distinction is important; this is who she has always been, even if we didn't know it for the first eleven years.

That was the beginning of our first media storm. It felt like the whole country wanted to talk to us. Reporters wanted a family angle on transgender issues, and we were willing to provide that in a way that was relatable. The media seemed to love how statistically average we were, beyond having a trans child.

I spent a lot of time correcting journalists' language and assumptions back then, and I often thought about how exhausting it must be for trans people to do the same. I could only imagine the invasive, embarrassing and downright insulting questions they had likely been asked over the years about their genitalia, surgery plans and sexual preferences.

For a long time, the public wanted nothing to do with the trans community. When people finally got interested, they were fixated on all the wrong things—things that didn't further the conversation or encourage acceptance. They wanted the shock factor. It took trans elders a lot of time and effort to begin steering society away from the idea of trans people being freaks or punch lines, and especially before trans children could be interviewed in a respectful way. Even then, I had to interrupt some questions. Children like Alexis should not be asked about their genitals. Nor should their mothers, for that matter, unless you want an earful on how inappropriate that is.

A friend who has a trans son put it well: if you wouldn't feel comfortable asking your neighbour, don't ask a trans person. And chances are you don't ask Dave from next door what his junk looks like or how he has sex. (If you do, we need to have a little talk about boundaries.)

The good news was that the world was changing. Laverne Cox, a trans woman of colour, made the cover of *Time* magazine. Caitlyn Jenner, former Olympian and current reality star, was speaking out about her own transition, as controversial as she could be. And families like ours were beginning to get positive press rather than being thrown to the wolves.

A few days after our interview aired, I heard my own voice

on the car radio. It seemed our documentary had gone national. I couldn't help but laugh. So much for blending in.

People all over the country, especially trans people and their families, began to contact us. "Thank you for speaking out for those of us who can't," one person said to me. "It's too dangerous where I live." Messages like that were a reminder of why we had shone a big, uncomfortable spotlight on ourselves. We were in a good position to do so. We had far more safety, security and support than a lot of people. It was vital to use our privilege to lift everyone up.

THIRTEEN

goals

I HAD BEEN EATING my feelings for as long as I could remember. Stuffing my face with complete abandon was a coping mechanism I had learned in early childhood. For a little while in my teen years, I all but stopped eating and instead used drugs and alcohol to cope. But once I got sober, I returned to a familiar lover, and since then, we had been going steady for decades.

Stressed out? Eat.

Feeling sad? Eat.

Excited? Oh, you guessed it, you smart (and likely delicious) cookie: eat.

I wasn't managing my anxiety disorder the way I should have. Instead, I was choosing to self-medicate with food.

But it wasn't just food. My whole lifestyle was unbalanced. I didn't make time to exercise—I didn't move very much in general—and I had put on a lot of weight over the past several years. I was nearing three hundred pounds. I'm not someone obsessed with being thin, but I was heavy enough I had health issues: sore joints, a bad back and steadily climbing blood pressure.

By February 2015, I had had enough. My health had started to worry me. I had a child who needed me to advocate alongside her, to be extra strong for her, and I wanted to be around for a long time to do just that. She and her brothers also deserved to have a parent who modelled confidence and self-love. But like many caregivers, I'd found reasons to neglect my own needs: life was busy; my children needed me; I had an article due; the dogs, the house, appointments. Life.

Enough of that. Why was I still my own worst enemy? I had to make myself a priority.

I decided not to do anything drastic; instead, I would try slow, simple changes that I could maintain. I would still eat what I liked, just less of it. I would exercise and try new things. I would gradually implement these changes instead of shocking my body with an alien new regimen.

Most importantly, I wasn't going to tie my success to the scale. I knew I would never be a small person without a great deal of sacrifice—and who wants to sacrifice things? I wanted my blood pressure to go down and my heart to stop racing, and I needed to find better tools to manage my anxiety. I wanted to replace some of the fat on my body with lean muscle mass, which I hoped would help my back and knees.

I joined a weight management clinic that shared my philosophy of being the best version of myself, rather than the version expected on a BMI scale or in a magazine. The team supported my desire for slow, incremental lifestyle changes, which I was already making, and helped me stay on track for the first few months. It was time. After years of feeling like I didn't deserve it, I was finally going to put myself first.

In early 2015, I also wrote my very last high school exam. Knowing I had aced it, I walked back to my car feeling on top of the world, closed the door and screamed excitedly. Eight different high school programs, so many obstacles, several failed attempts—and I had finally done it.

I was thirty-eight years old and I was going to get my diploma.

My friends threw me a surprise graduation party. They had me pose for cheesy photos and even made me a yearbook with all their baby-faced high school pictures in it. They took turns signing it with all the same ridiculous stuff teenagers sign in each other's yearbooks.

Graduation day was in June. The staff at St. Nicholas Adult High School went all out for their grads. We were in a beautiful auditorium, wearing caps and gowns, and were called out on stage in alphabetical order. My partner, children, siblings, parents and two close friends, Liliane and Angela, were in attendance. When my name was called, everyone cheered. "That's my mom!" Aerik yelled, doing his best to embarrass me.

Toward the end of the night, I was presented with the school's English award. I was floored. "Nobody is surprised but you," Angela whispered when I sat back down, still in shock and positively beaming with the plaque in my hands. After two decades, I was leaving high school in style.

It was a good time in my life. And the good just kept on coming. First, I got an email from the principal of our local middle school. She had heard our story on CBC and wanted to talk about bringing Alexis to the school for eighth grade. We were hesitant.

We knew that most of the kids who had been quick to drop or mock her would be at the same school. Alexis was just starting to get her confidence back, and we didn't want to put her through social hell again. But the principal assured us the school had a welcoming and inclusive environment. They would work hard to make her feel like a part of the community.

When we went to visit the school, we saw "safe space" stickers on every door. The principal, Shannon Smith, was kind, smart and extremely knowledgeable about trans issues. She took Alexis on a tour, and they bumped into a few of her former classmates along the way. Most of them greeted her excitedly, using the right name and pronouns. It's incredible what a difference a year and some education can make. Before long, Alexis had made up her mind to return to school in September.

I was also contacted by a member of the Pride Toronto staff and invited to that city's festivities that summer. We jumped at the chance and found a nice hotel downtown. The weekend was very rainy, but we still had a wonderful time at our first Pride event. At one point, my spouse got matching glitter butterfly face paint with Alexis. "Aww! Father-and-daughter bonding!" I said with a smile.

The incessant rain stopped just before the Pride parade, and the sun came out to shine some light on a gay ol' time. I looked over at my family with my own sense of pride; we had made it through a transition and were happier on the other side. My kids were pointing at floats, dancing to the music and just being in the moment. I seared it all into my mind.

FOURTEEN

revelations

IT WAS TIME to tell. But the girl from Peterborough didn't know how.

Pride had been her undoing. Seeing so many people out and proud, living their truths while she languished inside this life that wasn't hers, was too much to bear. Seeing her daughter thrive in a more authentic existence filled her with both happiness and piercing sorrow.

How much time had she already wasted? How much had she invested in trying to be the man everyone expected her to be? To be someone's husband, someone's dad, someone's son, someone's brother?

But terrified wasn't a strong enough word for how she felt at the thought of speaking this truth. There wasn't a word to convey what she was feeling in this moment. Terrified doesn't keep you in the closet for more than forty years, even when it's killing you to be in there.

What do you call it when the urge to be yourself is so strong that you can no longer contain it, but you know that you will likely lose everything you've worked for and everyone you love?

That feeling, right there. That was what this was.

She needed to find the right time to say something. In the meantime, it was eating her alive.

—

We returned from the Pride Toronto festival on June 30 and had a typical Knox family Canada Day weekend. We went to the Kanata street festivities with the kids, bought gross hot food on a gross hot day, paid way too much for carnival ride tickets, watched a C-list band perform as night fell, stayed for the fireworks and walked home. It was good. It was average. It was expected.

It was exactly the opposite of the following day.

July 2 is now another anniversary in our family. It's the day when everything changed—again. That was the night my partner and I went to Quitters, the coffee shop where I couldn't quit it. Despite the lovely ambience and great Americanos, I wouldn't let go of what was bugging me.

I needed to know what was happening in the mind of the person I lived with, raised children with, shared a bed with and had built an entire life with. Why the permanent Eeyore cloud? Didn't we deserve a chance to work through it and bring out the sun?

On the way home on that dark, rainy night, with the smell of air conditioning pouring in through the vents of our silver Cobalt and the sound of wipers squeaking against the window, I started gently pulling bricks from the wall between us. One, then another, with diligence and care. I didn't get annoyed or raise my voice. I tried to make room for whatever needed to be said. Finally, after all these years, it was time to get to the bottom of why it was as rainy inside the car as outside.

I started throwing out big questions—the ones I didn't really want the answers to.

"Are you unhappy with me?" I asked.

"No," came the response. "Not at all. I love you."

Gentle but direct. That was key.

"Is it our life, then? Is it the whole 'married with three kids' thing? Because I know we started young."

"No, not at all. I love our family. This predates you and the kids. It's nothing, okay? We don't have to talk about it."

Now I knew it was personal, not situational.

"Are you gay?" I asked.

"No. I don't like men," came the immediate reply.

For a while afterward, I wondered why I had asked the next question. Did I think it was impossible and just wanted to get it out of the way? Did I think it was a big enough reason for someone to be so unhappy? Did my subconscious already know the answer?

"Are you a woman?" I asked.

The answer came in the form of complete silence. All I heard were the tires rolling on wet pavement and the squeaky hum of the wipers moving back and forth, back and forth, wiping away the raindrops the way I wanted to wipe away the question.

Because now I knew.

The wall between us crumbled, and I saw what I had failed to see for more than two decades. I would spend the next few weeks wishing I had never asked, wishing I could take it back, wishing we could return to that snapshot in time at the Pride parade, back to my grad—hell, back to any time when I felt I had some control over my life. Because it sure didn't feel like that now.

"You—" I stammered. "You want to be a *woman*?"

Want to be. A terrible choice of words. I knew better. If my spouse was trans, she had always been a woman. But I wasn't thinking straight.

After what felt like a lifetime of waiting, I heard a faint frightened voice just above the rain and the drone of the engine.

"I can't talk about this." Eyes on the road, not looking at me, just driving into that dark, rainy night.

I was nearly speechless—which, if you ask anyone who knows me, is as rare as a trilingual unicorn.

"Y-you . . ." I tried again. "You're a *woman*?!"

"I said I can't talk about this right now," came the voice in the driver's seat again.

And I—a friend of the trans community, a voice of inclusion, a speaker of things in a positive light—answered with a poetic "Oh, you have got to be *fucking* kidding me!"

I hate telling that part of the story. It's just about the worst thing I could have said to her. Negative emotions eroded empathy. Instead of being a supportive wife, I had just kicked my spouse in the shins the moment she stepped out of that closet.

—

At this point, we were a few minutes away from pulling into the driveway.

"We can't go home now," I said, anxiety clinging to each word. "We can't go home like this. The kids are there."

The kids. The kids who thought they had a mom and a dad, and had just been through a big change a year before. Oh my God, the kids. All I could think about was them.

Instead of turning into our neighbourhood, she drove straight, seemingly on autopilot. Where do we end up on this road if we're not going home? Oh, right. Walmart.

She brought the car to a stop beside a lamppost in the parking lot, the light illuminating half her face. We sat in silence for a minute, not knowing where to go next with this conversation. For the second time in my life, I wondered where the instruction manual was for this particular situation. Even a pamphlet would do: *So Your Partner Came Out as Trans: A Starter's Guide*. That should be in every glove box next to the maps no one reads.

"I shouldn't have said anything," she offered meekly. "I'm so sorry, Amanda. I didn't know how to tell you."

"No, I'm glad you said something," I replied, and I partially meant it. I knew it must have caused her immense pain to carry that burden for so long.

But I was heartbroken for me. And angry for me too. Angry that she hadn't told me sooner. Angry that I had asked what was wrong many times before and been given any explanation but this. Angry that I had allowed myself to believe the dust had settled in our lives. I felt betrayed.

Yet I knew betrayal was not what this was. She hadn't deliberately misled me. For forty-two years, she had been trying to survive. But it was too soon to think clearly. My reasonable side was at war with my emotions, and my emotions were winning.

"I haven't been able to tell anyone this," she said, and my anger suddenly began to dissipate. "You're the first person I've felt safe enough to say something to in a long time."

"It's good you felt safe enough to finally tell me. I just don't know what to do now." I looked out the window and sighed. "What do we do?"

"I don't know," she said. "I wanted to say something, but I wasn't planning to tell you like this."

"I'm sure you weren't."

"I'm sorry. I'm really sorry."

"It's not your fault." I reached for her hand. "This is who you are."

"It's okay if you want to leave, you know," she said, her voice breaking, still not meeting my eyes. "If there was ever a time when you had a Get Out of Marriage Free card, this is it. I'll understand. You didn't sign up for this."

"Honestly, hon, I have no idea how I'm feeling right now. I need to process this. But no matter what, I support you in being who you are," I said.

She nodded sadly.

We sat in the rain and silence for a few minutes longer. "Let's go home and get some sleep," I said at last. "Try not to look upset in front of the kids, okay? Let's figure some things out before we tell them anything."

We got home that night and pretended everything was fine. I could have faked anything at that point. I had no emotions to speak of. I kept expecting to have a good cry and it wouldn't happen. I kept waiting to feel angry and want to smash things, but nothing came. The only feeling I had was a physical one in the pit of my stomach, gnawing at me, reminding me I had some big feels coming. Just you wait. Enjoy that numbness while you can.

We fell into bed, barely speaking. Neither of us knew what to say. I waited until I could hear she was asleep, then I reached for my phone and sent off a text to my friend Liliane.

"Hey, are you sleeping?"

"No," she fired back quickly. "Need to talk?"

I did. When Alexis came out, Lil was the first person I spoke to outside the family. Now, teary and terrified, I needed her again.

"Yeah, but let me call you in a minute. I'm going to walk down the street first."

I made my way downstairs, quietly slipped on my shoes and left the house. The rain had stopped but humidity hung thick in the air, a typical July night in Ottawa, sticky and uncomfortable. I dialled Lil's number, pacing.

"What's up?" she said. She could already tell it wasn't good.

"Uh, well . . ." I began. My voice was shaking. "Remember all those times I said I was glad it was my child who was trans and not my spouse, because I didn't know what I would do in that situation?"

"Yeah," Lil replied cautiously, waiting for the other shoe to drop.

"My husband just came out."

There was a long pause. "Wait. What do you mean, 'out'?"

"I mean he's actually *she*. She's trans too."

"What?"

"I don't think I'm supposed to tell anyone right now. But I'm telling you because if I don't say it out loud to someone, I'm going to lose it. How the hell does lightning strike twice in one family, Lil? I don't understand how this is happening."

"You know I'm with you," she said. "I was with you through everything Alexis went through, and I'm with you now."

"Thank you," I said. "I know."

If you find someone like this, hold on to her. These are the ones you can count on. Brené Brown, a renowned author and research professor, refers to people like these as stretchmark

For a little while, it was just my mom and me. Baby Amanda and mom, Elizabeth (1977).

The Trinque family in our backyard in Aylmer, Quebec. Left to right: Katie, Charles Sr., Michael, Amanda, Elizabeth, Charles Jr. (1988).

Newly sober and newly joyful teenage me (1992).

The girl who changed it all: Alexis's first public photo after coming out (2015).

Nervous and excited (mostly nervous!) to take the stage at WE Day Vancouver with Alexis in November 2016. (Photo credit: Microsoft Canada)

Alexis and I getting ready to speak at a conference about how to be a trans youth and how best to support one (2017).

Zoe's first day at work as herself. To say she was
nervous would be an understatement (2016).

Meeting with Prime Minister Justin Trudeau after the tabling of Bill C-16,
the Trans Rights Bill (2016).

A happier, more authentic family of five. Jackson, Zoe, Alexis, Aerik and Amanda at home in Kanata, Ontario (2016).

Alexis, Aerik and Jackson on a much-needed family getaway to Prince Edward County, Ontario (2017).

The couple selfies are abundant these days (2017).

The wedding we should have had became our 20th anniversary vow renewal in 2017.
Left to right: Zoe, Alexis, Aerik, Jackson and Amanda. (Photo credit: Danielle Donders,
Mothership Photography)

Vow renewal celebrations with our wonderfully supportive parents. Left to right:
Charles, Elizabeth, Amanda, Zoe, Elizabeth, Clifford. (Photo credit: Danielle Donders,
Mothership Photography)

It's (another) girl! Alexis and her best-friend-turned-sister, Ashley (2018).

friends. They're the ones who grow with you through everything and love you no matter what. Everyone needs a Lil.

That night, I slept poorly, my stomach in knots. When I woke up, *she*—I didn't know what to call her yet; did she have a name picked out?—was already awake.

"I didn't really sleep last night," she said. I knew the feeling.

It was Friday and she was at the tail end of her vacation time. I knew we were likely in for a day of talking and sorting things out. That seemed like a high priority to me, so I couldn't figure out why I was suddenly so angry. It took me a minute to realize that I was about to revert to a very familiar pattern.

Just a few weeks earlier, I had started a program at the weight management centre. I was diligently walking almost every day and going to strength-training sessions three times per week. Today was one of my scheduled classes. It would be completely understandable to blow it off this one time, right? I mean, the person I thought was my husband had just told me she's my wife.

But I was angry with myself at the mere thought of not going. To make myself the lowest priority, especially at this juncture, screamed "bad idea." This is where I would falter if I wasn't careful. If I skipped this session, I knew I wouldn't go back. I would fall right back into my old habits and routines.

"I have to go work out," I said in a tone that left no room for negotiation. "I'll be back in a bit and we can talk then." I threw on some workout clothes and walked out the door.

At the centre, I chatted with some women in the change room. We talked about the weather and a couple of good recipes someone had tried that week. I followed them into the gym and worked out for half an hour, doing push-ups, burpees, rows, crunches and mountain climbers. I laughed at the trainer's jokes and paired up with one of the guys for a team exercise, making conversation the whole time. I sang along to the music. From the outside, you would never know anything big had just happened in my life.

When the session was over, I went back to the change room and said goodbye to everyone. "See you next week!" I called with a smile. Smiling me walked past the front desk, waved to the admin assistant, strolled back to my car, sat down in the driver's seat, closed the door, took a breath and started to wail.

I had never heard that sound come out of me before. It was a primal, devastating, hopeless cry. I now know it as the sound I make when I believe my world has completely fallen apart.

FIFTEEN

aftermath

"OKAY, AMANDA. Bring it back, bring it back. You're okay."

That was me, talking myself down from all the wailing. I had to be my own therapist in that moment. Besides, what exactly would I say if someone gently tapped on the window to check on me? "Well, see, I have a really hard time with change because I have an anxiety disorder and a bunch of old trauma, and I was just starting to feel good about my daughter coming out last year, and me not realizing I was actually kind of transphobic, and having to learn how not be a terrible human about things I don't understand, and now I just found out I have a wife instead of a husband, and I feel like a terrible human all over again."

That would be a great way to get someone to slowly back away from the car. I was going to file that away for a handy occasion— like the next time I got pulled over for speeding.

I needed to unload to someone I trusted. Liliane was at work, and besides, she couldn't be my only confidante in a time of crisis. I had to call in the reinforcements. I composed myself just enough to send a text to my friend Sarah, the one who had welcomed me to Kanata two years earlier. She works in a school and was home for the summer with her kids. Sarah was a safe someone to tell news that could leave you sobbing in a Chevy Malibu Hybrid outside a weight management clinic.

Shaky fingers typed out a message on my phone. "Hey, I'm in a really bad place right now," I said. "Can I come over?"

"Of course!" she wrote back. "Come on over. I'll be waiting for you."

Sarah met me at the door, arms outstretched to welcome me into a hug, and I practically collapsed in her embrace. "Come on, I'm going to make you a coffee," she said kindly, leading me into the house. She knows me well—I never pass up a coffee.

Over the next two hours, she did all the right things. She listened supportively, and when I used up the box of tissues, she brought me another. And another coffee too.

Sarah understood the shock I was experiencing ("How did I miss this a second time?" "What are we going to tell the kids?"), but she had no problem with my spouse being trans. She was more concerned with the fact that I was reeling from the revelation.

In fact, no one I spoke to in the following weeks demonized my wife; instead, they fully supported her. But they also supported me by honouring where I was in this journey. And I was at the beginning, at the very hardest part, buried under waves of panic and uncertainty.

While I sat and talked to my friend, I wondered who *she* had to talk to. *She*, the person I'd thought I knew inside and out but didn't. *She*, the person I had built a life with but wasn't sure I could continue my life with. *She*, the woman I had left in our bed, all alone, while I sought comfort from others.

—

The girl from Peterborough had no friends to talk to. Not close ones, anyway. There was one long-time friend, the male half of a couple, who sometimes came over to play guitar. There were some co-workers she had lunch with, but they never did anything outside the office.

Her life did not involve closeness. Keeping everyone at arm's length was the way it had always needed to be. From the moment she'd realized she wasn't a boy, she built that wall, brick by brick, to seal herself in. Keeping who she was locked away took every bit of emotional stamina she had. If people got too close, they might see what she was hiding. She might say too much, let the wrong thing escape from her lips, and her protective wall would crumble to the ground. If anyone found out, she would lose everything. But self-preservation involved a huge sacrifice.

As she lay in bed alone that morning, she thought about what she was losing. The life she had built up—the wife, the kids, the house, the career—was now a pile of rubble at her feet. The wall was gone, and she lay bare with nothing to protect her.

She had never been so afraid and sad and free in her life.

—

I had to go back home. She needed me.

Feelings are stupidly messy, aren't they? I was angry with her and with the situation, but I was also worried sick at leaving her by herself at her most vulnerable. I needed to process what had been said, but I felt like a terrible person for doing so. Would I have wanted to be left alone after telling someone my biggest secret? How must she be feeling?

I get pegged as a "nice person" a lot, and the label makes me uncomfortable. There are times when I'm embarrassingly self-centred and oblivious to the needs of others. That morning was one of those times. So I wiped my tears, gave Sarah one last hug and climbed back into my Malibu for the shortest and longest drive of my life. I had to get home to the person I had made promises to in front of all our loved ones eighteen years before. The person with whom I had built a life and had babies. She needed me.

I just didn't know how to help her through this, or if she even wanted me to. I didn't know anything anymore.

The unknown. Unpredictability. Instability.

I have tricks for dealing with my anxiety, but none of them were working that day. I couldn't eat a thing. My body was unpleasantly humming from a mix of adrenaline and caffeine. My hands shook as I unlocked the front door, then shook more as I clutched the railing and ascended the staircase. I took a deep breath before opening the bedroom door, unsure of what I would find on the other side.

She was still in bed, lying in a fetal position, staring at the wall, our muted beige duvet pulled over her. She looked so small that my heart sank in shame for having left her alone.

"Hi," I said faintly, unsure of what to say at all. What are the talking points for the day after you find out your husband isn't your husband?

"Hi," she replied quietly.

"I had to get to my workout," I said awkwardly, with a hint of defensiveness.

"I know. I'm glad you went."

"That was a lot to take in last night," I said, switching gears.

She had yet to meet my eyes and showed no signs of doing so now, instead staring out our second-storey window to the quiet street below. "I shouldn't have said anything at all," she replied hollowly.

"I—" I began, and was interrupted by a knock.

"Mommy? Daddy?" Jackson's little voice came through the door. "Can I come in?"

Jackson burst in, jumped up and landed on the bed. "Hey, Dad!" he said, peeking under the covers with a grin. "Are you still sleeping, sleepyhead?"

There's a part in the movie *Love, Actually* where a married woman finds out her husband is having an affair. She's blindsided by the revelation, utterly devastated, but doesn't show it to anyone. She mentally pencils in moments to get real about it, to tell her husband she knows, to fall apart, to scream into a pillow. Then she composes herself, wipes her tears, puts on a smile for her kids and rejoins her family. The children remain oblivious to any marital turmoil, which is just the way she wants it.

I kept her image front and centre. If there was one thing we were not prepared to do yet, it was to let the kids in on what was happening. What would we tell them at this point, anyway?

"Did you have any breakfast?" I asked Jackson as he squirmed on the bed.

"Yeah, Aerik gave me cereal. I didn't want to wake Dad up."

Dad. That word was a punch to the gut. Was she their dad? When Alexis came out, it was apparent very quickly that she wasn't the boys' brother but their sister. Did the same rules apply with a parent? I couldn't wrap my mind around anything in its murky state, so I decided not to try. I went into *Love, Actually* mode.

"That brother of yours is pretty great!" I smiled. "How about I make you some lunch and we let Dad rest?"

"Okay!" he said, jumping out of bed and scooting downstairs as only an eight-year-old can.

"Let's go for another drive later and talk some more," I said to my spouse, who was still looking lost as she stared out the window.

"I guess," she replied from the bed. "Sure."

We drove around later that afternoon. The car was becoming a cocoon of sorts, shielding us from the outside world while we figured out what this metamorphosis would look like. It was quiet as we left the suburbs and made our way out into the awaiting Eastern Ontario countryside, the two-lane highway sandwiched by fields of corn and soy, not quite ready for harvest.

"I want to stress one important thing," I said, looking straight ahead at the dusty side road, my hands gripping the wheel tightly. I was trying not to cry. "No matter what happens, no matter where this leaves us, I want you to know I support you in being you one hundred percent. I will always have your back on that."

One of the gifts Alexis had laid at my doorstep was a deeper understanding of what being transgender meant. Long gone were the misguided ideas I'd held about confused and ill individuals seeking perverted pleasure. In their place came the knowledge that trans people are simply trying to lead the lives they were always meant to live. They were born one way, told they were another, and then did their best to fight their way back to authenticity, however they could.

I was not in doubt about my partner's authenticity. This was who she really was. I needed to step aside with my pile of feelings and let that process unfold. I needed to show compassion, understanding and support. As a loved one, that was my job, no matter how it might affect me.

"I don't have to do this, you know," she said to me.

"Do what?" I asked, although I already knew what she was going to say.

"Transition."

Sometimes after telling someone your deepest secret, you wish you could take it back. If she hadn't told me the night before, we wouldn't have been having this conversation. If I didn't know what I now knew, this would have been a drive in the country with two Starbucks lattes in the cup holders and a happy playlist full of cliché top-forty music from 2008. If she could go back and tell herself not to let the secret out, there wouldn't be two heartbroken lovers having a conversation neither of them wanted to have.

But my Chevy wasn't a DeLorean, and there was no going back in time. So what else could she do? Well, she could try to take it back. She could try to stuff herself back in the closet, sealing it shut again. We would both know, of course, but maybe we could pretend it never happened, and life could return to some semblance of normalcy.

But it wouldn't. It couldn't, and it *shouldn't*. We both knew that. She was desperately grasping for something to pull us out of the quicksand, to make everything right again. The problem was, it was never right to begin with. Denial is not what solid foundations are built on.

"Are you a woman?" I asked.

"Yes," she replied quietly. "I think so."

"Then how can you not live as one?"

"Well, I haven't so far, have I?"

"Yeah, and that's worked out *really* well," I said, every word coated in sarcasm.

I could sense her deflate even more at my reply and instantly felt bad about it. Of all the times, this was not the moment to be sassy.

I took a breath. "Sorry. I'm just trying to understand why you would even want to do that. Can you explain?"

"Because being who I am will hurt the people I love. It will hurt you and the kids."

"This isn't something you can just stuff back inside you," I said. "We both know that's not the case."

"I can try," she replied, sighing deeply. "I'm sorry. I'm really sorry. It was a mistake to say anything."

"No, it wasn't. I wish you had told me sooner, but it wasn't a mistake to tell me. It's good you did," I replied.

But it didn't feel good. Not good at all. We drove in silence for a while longer, distant farm silos the only observers of the pain trapped inside our metal cocoon.

SIXTEEN

shattered

MY MARRIAGE IS OVER.

That was the only firm thought in my mind. There were many things I didn't know—like how this revelation would play out in our lives—but I was sure I needed to find a divorce lawyer.

There was no way our marriage could survive something this big. Not after everything we had already been through. Maybe—and it was a *big* maybe—we might have been able to work through this if we had been more solid to begin with, if we had been happier together. After years of enduring a relationship that teetered between mediocrity and misery, however, I couldn't see a way to make this work. Transition can be tough in the best of situations, and we were certainly not in that. Healthier marriages broke up every day under far less stress.

I had years of pent-up resentment toward the person I'd known for so long as my husband. Years of wishing I had married someone who seemed to appreciate what we had. Years of trying to make things better. Years of wondering where the fun and engaging person I first met at a party had gone.

And my spouse? Well, she seemed to have nothing but years of unhappiness to draw from. Did she even know what happiness looked like? Was it something she could even feel under the right circumstances? Would living as a member of one of the most marginalized groups of people on the planet create that happiness for her, or would it only bring about a whole new kind of misery?

That was if she even decided to transition, of course. Some people don't. They fasten new hardware to the closet door and climb right back in to stay. From what I had learned in my brief time making friends in the community, it can be enough for some simply to acknowledge how they feel; they might not have a burning desire to transition, at least not yet. Most do have that desire, but they realize the losses in their lives would be too steep, or it would simply be too dangerous.

Knowing how unhappy my partner's life had been before, I was fairly sure she didn't want to go back into the closet. She might be afraid to transition, but I didn't think that would stop her.

Good.

Not necessarily good for me, I thought, *but good for her*. I didn't want anything to stand in the way of her living the life she was meant to live. We both knew that the life of father, husband and everyday white suburban man with a garage full of tools and a golf bag in the trunk did not fit. That life fit her about as well as my jeans from grade ten fit me. It was a mask she wore and clung to tightly with both hands so it wouldn't fall off. Now she had finally let it fall away.

But what if, out of fear, she returned to the closet? Would that make things okay between us?

No. It wouldn't save our marriage. It *couldn't* save our marriage. We would both know we were living in a fabricated reality. It might look like real life, but it could never be. It might be someone else's truth, but it wasn't ours.

This—all of this—broke my heart. It tore at my insides to realize that whatever happened from this point on, we'd be going our separate ways. From the night we met, at a party where all we could see was each other, to dividing up our assets and making custody arrangements. That's where we were now. I knew it. I felt it. And a flame that had been lit up inside my heart since that night in 1993 flickered for the final time and went out.

I didn't know where to go from here.

—

The problem with having three kids is they don't exactly provide a lot of opportunities to talk privately about the demise of a relationship. Not only that, but they're little empathy sponges who pick up on everything. There was so much to say and so little space to say it. Over the next few days, whenever we started talking in the kitchen, one of our little sponges would walk in, soak up the mood and ask what was wrong.

"Nothing," one of us would say. "We're just talking."

"Uh-huh," would come the reply, and concern would cloud that juvenile face.

We'd move to our bedroom and speak in hushed tones. "Look," I would start, "I've been doing some thinking . . ."

"I have too," she would say. "I just want you to know—"

There would be a knock at the door, followed by a "Can I come in?"

"Sure," one or both of us would call, quickly trying to cloak any stress in our voices. "We're just hanging out."

We would hastily plaster smiles on our faces, trying to look relaxed. Just your parents, chillin' on the bed. Nothing to see here.

I don't think they bought it—not even once. They knew something was wrong from the moment we walked in after our miserable date night; they just couldn't figure out what. We had no idea what to tell them because we still had no idea what to tell each other. We needed more time.

So we took it. Today, our kids would tell you that their parents were out of the house a lot in the summer of 2015. We took to the car as much as possible, making our way into the country or to Ottawa's Greenbelt, a stretch of nature filled with lush trails and wildlife. The Saturday after she came out to me, we drove out to one of the Stony Swamp trails and walked along its wide, family-friendly paths. It was sunny and warm, but without the usual humidity that plagues Ottawa in the summer months. Kids ran ahead of their parents, chasing birds and climbing on rocks, fearless and carefree. Everywhere I looked, couples walked together, enjoying each other's company. A young man and woman strolled hand in hand, her belly round and full with maternal expectation. A jolt of pain ran through me, a memory of simpler times. This is what I thought we had, what I thought we were: a man and a woman, making a family. I was wrong. Everything I thought I knew was wrong.

"I think you're right," my spouse said to me.

"About what?" I asked, still transfixed by the expectant couple.

"I need to go through with this. Transition, I mean."

I couldn't understand why my heart was sinking, except that hearing those words made it real. I could almost reach out and grab them floating through the summer air and hold them in my hand like palpable, painful truths. My spouse had been in hiding for a lifetime. She was going to transition now. Our kids were going to be hit with another big adjustment. Life as our family knew it was about to change—again.

I hurt for all of us, but especially for her. This wasn't going to be easy, and I knew I didn't have the strength to ride it out with her. I just didn't know how to tell her that yet.

I had once read that you should wait six months after any significant changes in your life to make big decisions. Don't move. Don't change jobs. Don't leave your partner. Just sit with it for a while, wait for the dust to settle and then see where you end up.

For some reason, amid all the floating clutter in my brain at the time, that piece of advice bobbed to the surface. Even if I felt like things were over—a statistical probability, according to the internet—now was not the time to make that decision. It wouldn't hurt to give things half a year. Our emotions would settle. We could focus on building up a friendship, free of resentment and full of support—a far better relationship than the one we had now. We could do this amicably, giving the children time to adjust to their new normal and ourselves time to build new lives on this fresh pile of rubble. Most importantly, it would allow my partner to start her transition without having to begin life as a single parent at the same time. She deserved better than that.

"So if you're transitioning, I guess you need a name," I said, as we walked under a patch of trees. "Have any ideas?"

"Well, a few." She smiled.

"Lay them on me," I said. "I'm ready!"

"I was thinking of Suki," she said.

I laughed. She didn't.

"What?" I asked, "No. Seriously? You're kidding me right now."

"What's wrong with Suki?" she countered.

"What *isn't* wrong with Suki? It sounds like a fifteen-year-old's name! Why is this your first choice?"

So much for being Non-Judgmental Amanda, here for you every step of the way. Apparently, I draw the line at names.

"There was a girl in my high school named—"

"Exactly my point!" This time, we both laughed. "I veto Suki."

"Wait! You can veto my names?" she asked, a false look of shock crossing her face.

"I can. It was in our vows," I said.

We came to a marshy area and stood watching jolly toddlers feed ducks.

"What about Michelle?" she asked.

"No, I can't be married to a Michelle," I said matter-of-factly.

"Why not? I could totally see myself as a Michelle."

"Ninety percent of the Michelles I've known have been total bitches," I explained.

"That can't be true. There are statistically far too many Michelles for them all to be terrible people."

"Not *all*," I countered, rolling my eyes for dramatic effect. "Just most. Like the girl who used to punch me in high school. Or the one at the house I was living in on Gloucester—she used to eat all my cheese and deny it."

"That's only two!"

"Look, every time I say your name, I'm going to remember face-puncher Michelle or cheese-stealer Michelle and sneer a little. Is that what you want? Do you want me to sneer when I introduce you to people?"

"You should meet more Michelles," she said. "You need some kind of exposure therapy."

"That exposure should not begin at home."

"Okay, picky one," she said, making a grand theatrical gesture with her arms. "What do you think I should name myself?"

"Oh, I don't really care," I replied. She gave me the finger. "Okay, I *do* care, but not as much as you might think. Just not Suki or Michelle. Oh! And could you try to stay away from 'A' names? We already have Amanda, Aerik and Alexis. Poor Jackson will feel totally left out."

"Finally, a legitimate veto." She thought for a moment. "How about Zoë?"

"I love the name Zoë!" I said. The aunt of my childhood friend Emmy had that name. She lived out West and used to come visit from time to time. I was always taken by her style, attitude and sense of adventure. Unlike her sisters, who'd stayed local, she had gone off to build a life for herself on the other side of the country, and from my young vantage point, she always seemed to come back with more self-assuredness than she'd had the last time. Zoë was a perfect name to start anew.

"I like it too," she replied. "And it's the furthest thing from an 'A' name." We high-fived. A few toddlers looked up at us.

"It suits you, Zoë," I said, smiling.

We turned and made our way back to the car, just me and Zoë, and I reached for her hand. It surprised both of us, but it also felt . . . right. I had held this hand for over two decades. But with relationship changes on the horizon, this might be one of the last times. The conflicting feelings of rightness and wrongness created a tug-of-war in my chest.

I took a breath and focused on what was in front of me, what I knew for certain.

Zoë. I had a wife named Zoë.

———

Zoë.

The girl from Peterborough had a name now. A real name that rolled off the tongue and felt right in a way her given name never had.

For so long, she had hidden from the world, vowing never to step outside her cocoon. Now, awake and aware on a sunny July day, she could almost hear her new name carried on the breeze. She had so much still to do and so many fears to overcome. But this day, in this moment, she was choosing to push forward and *live*.

She hadn't always wanted to live. Once, years before, she had run out into a snowstorm—bootless, coatless—away from a late-night argument and her wife's insistence that she tell her what was wrong. She had almost spoken the words "I'm not a man!" out loud, and the proximity of that truth was too much to bear. So she ran, leaving the door wide open, tears streaming down her face, hoping to outrun the woman inside her just as she had once tried to outrun the girl within. She wanted to run far and fast, to freeze in the frigid Canadian landscape, to die of exposure, to fall peacefully and permanently asleep, to never come home. She could hear her name, the man's name that didn't fit, being shouted from the doorway, almost lost in the howling wind.

Aerik was a preschooler at the time, and in that moment, Zoë believed he would be better off without someone who could never truly be a father to him. She believed her young wife would be better off meeting someone new, someone less broken to build a life with. She didn't want to be alive in this prison she had built for herself—the one society had insisted would bring her joy.

Reason got the better of her and she returned home before frostbite set in. I stood at the door with tears in my eyes. "I was so worried about you. Why did you do that? We need you."

The next day, she tried to resume life as normal. Denial slowly buried the truth. It would take many more years and a talk in a parking lot to start to feel right.

Zoë: the most powerful two syllables she had ever spoken. She could finally be the girl she always knew she was.

Zoë, holding her wife's hand in the sun.

———

"I'm surprised it took you as long as it did to figure it out," Zoë said to me while we were making dinner that evening.

"I didn't figure it out," I said, stirring the taco seasoning into the pan. "I guessed."

"Did you, though?" she asked. "It's a weird thing to just guess."

"Not when we have a trans child."

"Maybe. Or maybe you knew but didn't want to look at it?"

I stared at the sizzling pan of ground beef as memories of the past two decades played in my mind like old movies.

Flashback: Her, as "him," standing awkwardly in a group of guys at one of the few parties we had hosted back then. I could see she was feigning interest, trying to make conversation on topics she cared little about. She held her body stiffly, looked uncomfortable and awkward. Why did my partner have such a hard time relating to my friends' partners? It always set us apart from them, and I was sure it was one of the reasons why we weren't invited to a lot of couples' get-togethers.

In the kitchen, where the women had gathered to make small talk and snack on appetizers, I blended in easily with my friends. After glancing over at us a little too often, my partner told the guys she was going to grab more chips and made her way into the kitchen, where she lingered outside our circle of women. She laughed at some of our jokes, made a few comments and visibly loosened up for a short while. And then, like a light suddenly being switched off, her body tensed again. She turned away, refilled the empty chip bowl she had been carrying and made her way back into the living room to rejoin the testosterone-charged group she had been told she was a part of for life. The men were talking hockey now, rather loudly, and that uncomfortable look with the fake smile crept back onto her face.

I had always known she wasn't one of the guys. I just didn't know to what extent.

Another flashback: We were in our current home a year ago, watching the *My Little Pony* reboot with the kids one weekend.

"This show is so good," she said. "I'm kind of a fan."

I thought she was saying it for the benefit of our youngest. I've always called Jackson our Little David Bowie. He identifies as a boy but could often be more fluid in his presentation and preferences when he was younger. He loved having his nails painted (I once wrote a blog post about this that made its way onto NBC's *Today* show) and thought high heels were great. But as he got older, peer pressure seeped into his world and he started to push out some of the more "feminine" things. I thought Zoë, still presenting as his dad, was trying to lead by example. So I joined in.

"I love that you're a fan. It says a lot about a man when he can say he likes something and not care what other people think."

"So you're a brony!" Jackson declared. "That's what they call guys who like the show."

"I guess, sure," Zoë mumbled, suddenly tense. The rain cloud was forming again.

I found her response a bit odd but chalked it up to a dislike of the title, not a dislike of how the world saw her.

I remembered another occasion a few years earlier. She was cutting the grass of our half-acre lot in the scorching heat. First the lawn tractor, then the mower, then the trimmer. It was a job she never looked forward to doing. Most guys I knew loved yard day. It involved a couple of cold beers, good music and some time alone with their thoughts. I remembered my dad escaping into yard work and seemingly enjoying every sweltering minute. But I tried not to stereotype; not all men like the standard masculine things. I already knew I was the one with the spouse who didn't like hockey or golfing or going out on the boat to drink beers and catch fish. Why should cutting the grass be any different?

"Just take your shirt off!" I called out the front door. "It might be less awful in this heat if you did!"

"No, I'm fine!" she called back over the lawnmower, pushing and pulling it in and out of the ditch in front of our house.

"I don't get it. Why not? It's one of the nice things about being a guy. I can put some sunscreen on you. I'll go get it, okay? You'll feel so much better!"

"*I said I'm fine!*" she yelled back, a little too harshly. "Just drop it. I'm good. Thanks."

I stepped back into the house, wondering what I had done wrong.

And then I remembered the Pride parade, when Zoë and Alexis got those matching face paintings: purple sparkly butterflies. I thought she was being a modern dad.

She was trying to tell me, "This is who I am. This is who I've always been. I'm just like her. Why can't you see that?"

No, I truly had no idea until that night at Quitters. I wasn't looking for it and I never suspected. I asked the right question, that's all.

Now everything was starting to make a lot more sense. It was like watching a movie when you already know the ending.

—

I have a close circle of five female friends. They had all known each other for years before I turned up, but I was still welcomed into this group of funny, eclectic, good-hearted people. We had a routine of meeting on Wednesday mornings in a food court at a local mall. It's an awkward place to tell your friends that your husband is, in fact, your wife.

When I had confided in them about Alexis, their immediate response was to offer unconditional support. They were kind and comforting at a time when others were walking away. I counted myself lucky to have them as friends.

But with Zoë coming out too, I wondered how much change

this circle could take. How would we be viewed now, as a family with two transgender people in it? Would friends be able to wrap their minds around that as easily as they had Alexis's situation? Would these women love us through it a second time, or would I be picking up a box of comfort crullers on my way out of the mall? Did they taste as good behind a steering wheel while sobbing?

I hoped not to find out.

The food court was busy that morning. I grabbed a coffee and sought out a quieter area. I sat on a hard white chair and breathed deeply and mindfully, enjoying the relative solitude and anonymity of a mall full of people. I had come to relish alone time. With the kids home for the summer, I had to wear fake smiles all the time, and I was walking on eggshells around Zoë, not wanting to make her feel worse about something she couldn't help. Leaving the house whenever I could became a necessity. It meant I didn't have to pretend that everything was fine, that *I* was fine. I used work as a guilt-free excuse—I was writing for a large online parenting publication, and I penned articles at Starbucks under the guise of needing a disruption-free environment.

"But your room is quiet," Alexis would say quizzically. "Quieter than Starbucks, for sure."

But Starbucks had lattes with extra foam and no emotional load. It had genuinely happy people in it, which made me genuinely happy, if only for a few minutes. I just couldn't explain that to her.

And I still didn't know how to explain this big life change to my friends. One by one, they trickled into the food court. We greeted each other with hugs, grabbed food and drinks, and settled down to make small talk. I tried to take in this moment, the laughs and inappropriate jokes, the complaints about someone's tween not getting up for school on time, the lament about how messy someone else's house was. It was so normal, so everyday, with typical struggles and typical complaints—a stark contrast to how I felt in my own life right now. I missed caring about how messy my house was.

"You've been pretty quiet," one of them said to me after a while. "What's new with you?"

The spell broke, the moment of blessed ordinariness fell away, and I was now staring at five faces I had grown to love.

"My husband came out to me," I said, ripping off the bandage. The smiles hung for a second, then dropped at the realization of what I had just said. "It seems I have a wife."

There was a pause. Then one of them said, "Oh, honey. What happened?"

I spilled it. The pain and fear of the past several days poured out of me: the trip to Pride, the parking lot conversation, all the worry I had been holding in about how this was going to change our lives. "She could lose her job," I said. "And how are her parents going to take things? And oh my God, the kids are going to be devastated." I spoke quickly, feeling light-headed, my breath shallow.

They leaned in closer.

"That's a lot to deal with," one of them said. "I can only imagine how she's feeling. And it's going to be a shock to the kids. But how are *you*? Are you okay?" she asked, looking in my eyes. The empathy was palpable. I had to look away so I wouldn't cry.

My hands shook as I stared down at them. "I don't think I can do this. It's too much. I can't," I said softly, my voice breaking. "I want to, but I can't."

"It's okay," another friend said.

"I love her," I continued. "I'll always love her. But I don't know if I can be *in* love with her. I don't think we've known love in a healthy way for a long time as it is. So many things are going to change, and I don't know if I'm strong enough to keep up."

Someone reached for one of my shaking hands, but I don't remember who. I just remember how much it meant to me.

"My marriage is over," I said, the tears finally hitting me in the middle of a freaking mall. "My marriage is over, and I don't know what to do."

Anyone walking by the Mexican stand that morning would have noticed a group of five women closing ranks around one, their arms around her shaking shoulders, holding both her hands and telling her things were going to be okay. Love in action.

—

Surrounded by work colleagues, Zoë was invisible that morning. As she walked down the hall from the cubicle farm on the fourth floor to the coffee station, she was greeted by polite nods and good-mornings along the way. Still, she felt unseen.

They didn't see her because they didn't know she was there. They had no clue about the life-changing revelation she'd made. They had no idea how she saw herself, had *always* seen herself. They didn't know she was a woman, and instead saw before them a familiar man with a slight build, shaved head, dark bushy eyebrows and two-day-old stubble. They saw someone but not her. She was invisible to them in the most important of ways: her identity, the core of who she was.

She had loved computers her entire life and had been encouraged by her parents to follow her passions. As a teenager, she built systems from spare parts after school and on weekends.

She worked on a neighbouring sheep farm for an entire summer to get enough money to buy a state-of-the-art computer on which she could code more powerful programs. She was the youngest member of the Peterborough Tech Enthusiasts Club.

Computers also gave her a way to hide. Even with the invention of dial-up modems, which allowed users to connect to and chat with others, you could still hide behind a screen; your name and identity could be anything you wanted. Zoë, the girl Peterborough knew as a boy, loved technology because it was interesting, but also because it allowed her to bend the rules, to play female characters in games and to escape society's expectations of her.

After a rough few years of attempted self-destruction, Zoë eventually decided to try to build a life again. At nineteen, she landed in Ottawa, where she studied computer science and scored the best internships. She'd been working at a global telecommunications company for the past twelve years, managing a team of software developers.

She felt like she knew everyone there. She felt like nobody knew her.

High-tech is still a male-dominated field, and Zoë knew her abilities had been more easily recognized and rewarded because of her perceived gender. She had set goals for five, ten, even fifteen years from now, and wondered how living outwardly as a trans woman—one of the least-respected and lowest-paid demographics—would affect that. Some trans people are dismissed from their jobs when they come out, even though there are laws against that very sort of discrimination. Some feel forced out due to intolerance or even outright aggression in the workplace; they simply can't continue working in a hostile environment. Employment rates and earnings among trans people are some of the lowest in the country. As the primary breadwinner in the family, Zoë worried deeply about this. If she lost her job for being herself, what would happen to the life we had built?

For now, her job was as secure as it had ever been. But the genie was out, and soon she would be too. What would that mean for her future?

"Hey, man," one of her colleagues said as he walked by her in the hall.

"Hey," she replied, smiling faintly.

Seen, but invisible.

SEVENTEEN

dissolution

I WANT TO go on record as saying that I tried really hard to be a supportive partner in the first few weeks after Zoë came out, and often failed miserably. *Miserably*.

An internal war was unfolding—one I now call the War of Two Amandas, an epic struggle that will likely be turned into a movie one day. Logical Amanda (played by Gillian Anderson, obviously) understood why Zoë needed to outwardly live as Zoë after years of suppressing her. And she knew why Zoë hadn't told her before. The tipping point for trans rights was *now*, in 2015, and not five, ten or twenty-two years ago. People were slowly arriving at a place of tolerance for, if not outright acceptance of, transgender people. It was starting to become easier to find good medical support, to change names and gender markers on ID, to be recognized and respected by people you know and to finally live life as the person you are.

Zoë had also seen the love shown to Alexis when she came out. She had been embraced by family, friends and neighbours.

Not everyone was on board, but it was enough to form a giant support circle around her. It was something Zoë had never thought possible in her lifetime, and it was both a comfort and a catalyst for her own transition.

Then there was Emotional Amanda (played by Kate Winslet, who could totally pull this off), ruler of Cruller Kingdom. She was the unfortunate relative to my logical side, the blundering monarch in a folklore tale. Even though her heart was in the right place, she said and did all the wrong things.

Emotional Amanda couldn't see the big picture. She couldn't understand why her partner had kept this secret for two decades. She was sadness with a face, anger with language, heartbreak with lungs.

"Hey, girl. Maybe you should let me handle this," Logical Amanda would gently suggest, guiding Emotional Amanda to a comfy spot on the couch. "I don't think you're . . . uh, equipped right now. How about I make you some tea?"

But Emotional Amanda couldn't just sit down. She didn't want tea. She was frantic, panicked and fighting to understand.

"How could you not tell me?" Emotional Amanda said to Zoë on more than one occasion, blame flying out of her mouth.

"You know why," Zoë would say. "There was never a good time."

"Right. Because when is a good time to tell me you're not who I married?" I would shoot back venomously.

"I *am* who you married. I'm still the same person. But I know what you're saying and I'm sorry. I can't tell you how sorry I am. I'll say it a million times if I have to."

She *was* sorry. Logical me knew it. How could I feel angry when I thought about everything she would have faced had she transitioned back then, and everything she was facing even now? But the anger would surge back unpredictably. I could be sweet and supportive one minute, withdrawn and bitter the next. It was the world's worst roller-coaster ride for both of us, and I didn't know how to stop it.

There is no guide for what to do when your partner of many years comes out to you. How do you navigate their feelings alongside your own? How do you honour your feelings when you know they're dealing with something bigger than you can imagine? How do you support that person when you don't know if you can get through this yourself?

I grappled with feeling betrayed, even though I knew this wasn't really a betrayal. I struggled with anger, even though I knew full well that anger was merely a mask for the fear and pain I wasn't ready to deal with yet. I wrestled with resentment, even though it made the supportive role I was trying to play much harder.

I didn't recognize this side of me and wondered just how much I had come undone to behave this way. I sometimes fantasized about dying—about running my car off a bridge or into a pole—but those fantasies were short-lived. My mind always rushed back to how the kids and Zoë needed me. In place of those dark thoughts, I would daydream of checking myself into a hospital for a few days, dazed and incoherent, so I could sleep and regain my strength.

I felt as if I were coming apart, and I hated myself for it. I expected better of me. This just made me angrier and more frightened, and it fuelled the emotional roller coaster. You know what makes awful feelings even worse? Feeling bad about those awful feelings.

I recently asked Zoë to tell me how I did in those early days. She said, "Well, you tried," in the nicest way she could.

I tried. That about sums it up.

———

I still didn't want to tell her it was over. I wasn't ready to face that, and I was sure she wasn't either. Zoë had many things to do before she could come out to the world, and they would take all her strength. I wanted to give her the emotional room to do those things. Also, although it surprised me to be thinking it, a part of me hoped I might come to a different conclusion about where we were headed as a couple. Even though everything about our marriage was bleak and grey, I had moments when I envisioned us miraculously working through it all and coming out the other side.

For the moment, however, it all felt fake. Not only the wedding pictures of what seemed like a hopeful young bride and groom with a baby in their arms, but the entirety of our lives together so far. The day we met, the day we wed, the babies we brought into the world and the dreams we had for the future. The very house itself—every wall, every toy, every throw pillow on our bed. Looking at it was looking at a life I had bought into, believed in, when it wasn't what it appeared to be.

I needed time to sort through the rubble, to make sense of what I was seeing and to solidify it in my mind as a new reality. I didn't want to cry whenever I looked at our throw pillows (they're really cute pillows), and judging by how I was doing at the moment, that was going to take some work. Meanwhile, Zoë had to find the supports necessary to begin socially and medically transitioning. Two big, life-changing projects by two people overloaded by life itself.

—

We began leading parallel lives. We didn't do it on purpose—we just fell into it. It was simpler than figuring out what came next for us; we first needed to figure out where we were going as individuals. We still lived together, slept in the same bed, talked a lot and tried not to argue. I did my best to keep Emotional Amanda on a tight leash. We were both raw and sad, and trying to hold ourselves together for the kids. They still didn't know anything. We both knew we had to tell them soon. But because we hadn't sorted out where we were heading as a couple, we wouldn't be able to answer the question we knew they would ask: Are you getting a divorce?

We had rallied together in the most beautiful way when Alexis came out, making our family seem stronger than ever. I wasn't ready to tell them we wouldn't be getting through this one intact. It broke my heart to even think about that conversation.

I know people get divorced all the time. I know families split up, assets are divided, tears are shed, papers are signed and life eventually moves on. Both adults and children often find happiness beyond the breakup. It feels like the end of the world at the time, and then one day you realize it's just the start of something else. But I don't know a single person who has taken divorce lightly, especially when kids are involved. We needed time. We wanted to set the course that would be healthiest for all of us.

Zoë knew what she needed to do. There was both a medical route and a legal route she had to follow to be recognized as the woman she had always been. But the process for each was long and piled high with obstacles. "Have some patience," those who had been through the process were telling her. She had met some trans people through a local support group. Zoë had been reluctant to get to know people in the trans community when she was still hiding from herself and everyone around her. Their genuineness was too uncomfortable when she wasn't living genuinely herself. Now she was grateful for their guidance and friendship. To see people further along in the process was both inspiring and frustrating. She could see where she wanted to be, but she was nowhere near there yet.

There was one local health clinic that had become the hub for adult trans-related health care. Services were free of charge, but the wait was long—six months at least. That was just to be seen by the clinic psychologist, who would need several appointments to make the assessment required to get to any next steps, like hormone blockers, hormone replacement therapy or surgery. When Zoë called the clinic, the staff apologized for the long wait but said they had recently been swamped by referrals.

Six months just to begin the process felt like an eternity. She had already waited forty-two years. The idea of being stuck in a holding pattern was anxiety-producing, to say the least. She knew her mental health would take a nosedive.

No, this needed to happen sooner.

But her friends in the know urged her to settle in, to celebrate the small steps while she waited for the big ones. They reminded her that this was a marathon—not a sprint—and it would take time. This advice came from experience.

Another piece of advice she got was to start putting money away because her wife was likely going to leave. She needed to prepare herself.

"I don't know if she will," Zoë said, when confronted with the idea. "She's surprised and upset, but she's been really supportive of my transition."

Many in the local community knew of the advocacy work I did as the parent of a trans child. But still, they argued, Amanda's human. It's different when it's your partner. You're not her child. She doesn't love you unconditionally. She might not even be attracted to you when you present as a woman. Have you thought of that? Maybe you'll discover you're not attracted to her either. So many things can change, you know. You should be cautious. We say this only because we care.

These were fair statements. Many people had been through bad breakups. Some were estranged from their children. A few had partners who stayed, but the partners sometimes had strict rules about what was acceptable if their relationship was to survive: You can talk about your desire to transition, but that's as far as it goes. You can live as a woman, but only at home and not in front of people we know. You can medically transition with blockers and hormones, but you can't get any gender-affirming surgeries. The trans partner had to compromise who they were to stay with the person they loved.

None of those situations would work for Zoë. She knew what she needed to do to feel whole. She tried to remain hopeful, but doubt crept in. Maybe her wife wouldn't be able to ride through this. Maybe her temporary distance would become permanent.

It was time to face that head-on.

—

We had exactly one big fight in the first few weeks. It took place in the kitchen, and there's still a hole in the wall from when it ended.

It was a sunny August weekend. Aerik had taken Alexis and Jackson to the public pool. I was cleaning the kitchen and trying not to think about anything but unloading the dishwasher. I find dishes very therapeutic when I'm anxious. We never have a cleaner kitchen than when I'm in the midst of a crisis.

Zoë was hovering around, sorting recycling and putting things away. Ever since that night in the car, she had barely left my side when I was home. It was one of the reasons I went out as much as I did: her need to be close only fuelled my guilt. Some days, I wanted to run as far and as fast as I could.

I also found the experience odd. For years, Zoë had been the one to sequester herself from the rest of the family. She built a music studio/office in the basement of our old home and would spend hours down there by herself. In our current home, which was too small for a studio, she would spend hours at her desk in the family room writing software, toying with an operating system or coming up with a new bassline for a song. It's not that she didn't spend time with us—she did—but there was some reluctance to it. In retrospect, I can see that the dad and husband role was so ill-fitting, so uncomfortable, that she needed to avoid it whenever possible.

But now she was ever-present. When I was home, she wanted to talk, watch TV, take a walk or just be in the same room as me. I had often longed for this kind of couple time, but now I wasn't able to appreciate it.

"Hey," Zoë said, turning to look at me that day in the kitchen. "Are we okay?"

I broke out of my thoughts, jarred by the suddenness of the question. There was no lead-up, no small talk before getting to the big stuff. I felt the air in the room go cold.

"I don't really want to have this talk right now," I said. "I don't think it's a good time." I loaded cups into the dishwasher, aligning them as carefully as I was trying to avoid this conversation.

She didn't let go. "This is important. We need to talk about it."

"What do we need to talk about? The fact that you're transitioning, and I'm supposed to have all the answers to what that means?"

Uh-oh. Enter Emotional Amanda, ready to drama things up and with no doughnuts in sight to appease her.

She was in good company. Emotional Zoë had stepped up to the plate too. It was a side of her I wasn't used to seeing. She had stuffed her feelings down for so long that they bubbled up only as frustration and anger. In the past few weeks, she had expressed a depth of emotion that surprised me. She would get sad or scared instead of immediately angry. She would even cry, which I had seen her do only a handful of times.

"I just need to know we're okay," she said. "That we're going to get through this. Or that we're not. I hate not knowing. I hate it. I'm on pins and needles with you all the time lately. It's hard."

"This is hard too!" I shot back, waving my arms to show the scope of what I was trying to manage: our life, our family, us. "I'm exhausted, okay? I barely get through each day!"

"You think it's easy for me?" she asked.

"No, but at least you're getting something out of it. You get to be you. What do I get? To find out my relationship is a lie?"

"How is our relationship a lie?" she asked, hurt mounting in her voice.

"You know what I mean," I replied, sitting down with a thump at the breakfast bar. She sat across from me. My pulse was racing.

"This isn't a lie, Amanda," Zoë said. "We are not a lie. What we have is built on love. That hasn't changed. We're still the same people. *I'm* still the same person."

"I didn't get a say in this, you know," I said, my eyes filling with tears. "I'm just expected to go along with it. How is that fair?"

"I didn't get a say in this either," she said. "I can't help who I am."

"I know," I said softly, looking down.

"And no one is expecting you to go along with it. I've told you from day one, I'll completely understand if you leave. You didn't ask for this. I know." Tears ran down her face.

This was it. This was the moment for me to tell her it was over. I could walk away free and clear. What was there left to build on, anyway? Our very foundation was blown apart. We could chart a healthier course, building up a friendship from here and learning how to co-parent. No more fighting, no more avoiding. All I had to do was say the words.

I couldn't. They were stuck in my throat, clinging fiercely to the sides, knowing they couldn't be unsaid once I spoke them. How do you say something when it will mean the end of the life you've built?

But Zoë wasn't waiting any longer. She wasn't going to live in limbo. "Are we done?" she asked, looking me directly in the eyes.

I took a deep breath. Out came the words: "I think we are, yeah."

"Fuck!" she cried. She picked up her phone and threw it as hard as she could at the wall behind the kitchen counter. She then left the room, sobbing.

There's still a hole in the wall from when that chapter of our lives ended. It's right by the kitchen sink. I can't bring myself to patch it up yet.

EIGHTEEN

solicitude

WE DIDN'T TALK much for the next couple of days, save for Zoë apologizing for throwing her phone at the wall. She felt that I had just set her last shred of hope on fire. I felt like the destroyer of lives and kicker of people when they're down.

I also felt no relief at saying the words I had been holding back. I had expected to feel terrible, yes, but in that relieved, at-least-I-finally-said-it kind of way. Instead, I only felt terrible. I wasn't planning a life beyond this marriage. I wasn't working out budgets or thinking of living arrangements. I wasn't working on ways to tell the kids. I was just sad.

This was confusing, to say the least. Telling Zoë it was over didn't feel like the first step in moving forward. It felt like the first wrong step on the wrong path. But staying in the marriage didn't feel right either. There was too much resentment, too many emotions tied to a transition happening two decades into our coupledom. All I knew right then was that my decision didn't seem final to me.

I found Zoë folding laundry in the basement. "Hey," I said, "can we talk for a minute?"

"Sure, I guess," she replied, not taking her eyes off the pile of towels in front of her.

"Look, I'm sorry for what happened the other day. I'm sorry for the way I've been acting. There's no excuse for some of the things I've said." *Deep breath, Amanda. Keep going.* "I know what you're going through is hard, but it's been hard for me too. I have so many mixed emotions, and I don't know how to deal with them all."

"Of course you have mixed emotions," Zoë replied softly, meeting my eyes. "I've had most of my life to think about this and I'm still a mess. You've had only a few weeks."

"Thank you," I said, grateful for her understanding. "I don't want to make this about me. I really don't. But my feelings are all over the place right now. I just need some time to sort through everything. Can we please give it some time?"

"Yes, we can," she said. "That's what I want too. I'm sorry I pressured you. Let's hit pause on this 'figuring things out' business and see what happens, okay?"

I was shaking. She put down the towels and hugged me.

Zoë—the real Zoë beneath the masculine mask—is a loving, caring person. In that moment, in our messy laundry room with its bad fluorescent lighting, I started not only seeing the positive effects of her coming out but feeling them too. This was a depth of love I hadn't felt from her before, and I was surprised by how much it moved me. Her simple act of compassion was an ember in a fire I thought had been completely snuffed out. It was the beginning of something new.

I didn't yet know what this newness looked like, but for the first time, I wanted to stick around a little longer to find out.

"Mom, what's going on?" Alexis asked while I was making dinner a few days later. "Why have you been crying so much lately?"

"I'm fine, sweetie," I said. "I've just been dealing with a few things."

"Are you and Dad getting a divorce? That's what we think."

They were on to us. They knew something was wrong, and with no facts to draw from, they were coming up with their own theories.

"We're all really worried," Alexis said. "Could you just tell us what's happening?"

"I'm going to need to talk to Dad first, okay?" It was weird calling her "dad." I hope that didn't show on my face. "I'll see if he can come home a little early. Let's all sit down together and have a talk."

Alexis looked even more worried after that, but she agreed and left the room, presumably to go tell her brothers they were right about there being big problems between their parents.

I shot Zoë a text: "Hey, I think we need to tell the kids. They're asking questions. Can you come home ASAP?"

"Okay. I'll pack up right now. See you soon," came the reply.

Shit-shit-shit-shit-shit. Adrenaline hit me hard, almost knocking me over. I went into a full-blown anxiety attack.

I had been dreading this moment. It's one thing to tell your kids they have a sister, but to tell them they have two moms is an entirely different matter. I was quite sure Zoë wasn't looking forward to it either.

Aerik, Alexis and Jackson were all seated nervously in the living room, awaiting the big news we were about to share.

"I'm trans," Zoë stated. "I'm a woman. I've always known I was a woman—I just didn't let myself think about it. I stuffed it deep down and hid it from everybody, including me. What this means is that like Alexis, I'm going to need to start living as myself." She delivered the news in a calm, measured way.

There was a pause while our children absorbed what they had just heard.

Then finally, a small eight-year-old voice said, "You mean, I don't have a daddy?"

Jackson's composure crumbled at the realization and he began sobbing into his little hands, kneeling on the floor. A piece of his own identity, something he knew for sure—that he had a mom and a dad—had just changed forever.

I started to get up from the couch and hug him, but Aerik was there in a heartbeat. He wrapped his long, big-brother arms around his weeping little brother.

"It's okay, buddy," he said tenderly, as a tear slipped down his own face. "It's going to be okay."

Alexis was crying too.

"Are you all right?" Zoë asked her.

"I know they're both crying because they're sad," she said. "I understand why. But I'm just so happy for you. I know what this means. I know what it took for you to do this. You're going to feel so much better."

The wisdom of lived experience poured out of a twelve-year-old girl. Zoë reached out and held her hand.

For the second time in less than two years, I watched change hit our family. There was fear, uncertainty and sadness. But more than anything, what I saw was unconditional love and support. People being there for each other, even while trying to process a dramatic revelation. In that moment, I knew our kids were going to be just fine. How could they not be? With love, compassion, understanding and resiliency, they had every tool they needed to move into our new normal.

"I'm sure you have questions," Zoë said. "You can go ahead and ask them."

"What does this mean for our family?" Aerik asked, letting go of his little brother and taking a seat on the sofa again. "Are you two splitting up?"

Zoë looked at me to answer. Fair enough. She knew what she wanted, and that was us. The decision came down to what *I* wanted.

I didn't want to lie to them; that wouldn't be fair. If I said something to appease their worries now and told them something different down the road, I would only be prolonging their pain. No, I had to be honest with them. For the past few weeks, my gut had been telling me it was over. What was it saying now? I searched deep, excavating what I felt, and laid it out for them.

"That's not the plan," I said, surprising myself a little. "We have a lot to figure out, but we love each other." I smiled at Zoë, who smiled back with a subtle look of surprise. Relief filled our children's faces.

I had come back around, through shock and sadness and anger, to a place where I was willing to give it my all. I still didn't know what that meant, but I knew where my heart was: here, with the people in this room.

Jackson was still on the floor, wiping his tears. Zoë got up from her chair and moved over to him.

"Buddy," she said softly. "I'm sorry I'm not your dad. I know that's a big realization, and it's okay if you're angry about it."

"I'm not angry," he said. "I'm sad. I thought I had a dad."

"I know you did," she replied. "But you still have two parents who love you. That hasn't changed, right?"

"Right," came the reply. "I just don't know what you are to me now."

"Well, I'm a woman just like Mom" she replied, rubbing his back. "So I guess that makes me your other mom."

"Okay," he said, taking it in. He hugged her.

"That's my next question," said Aerik. "What do we call you? Mom is already Mom."

"What about Mama?" offered Alexis. "Like on *The Fosters*." She had turned all of us on to that show. It was a heartwarming teen drama about a same-sex couple raising a mix of biological, adopted and fostered children. One of the mothers was called "Mom" and the other "Mama."

"I like it," said Zoë.

"That works," the other two agreed.

They then asked her if she had a name picked out for herself.

"I'm going with Zoë," she said, smiling. "Zoë Michelle Knox."

"Nice," said Alexis.

"I tried to talk her out of the Michelle part." I rolled my eyes.

"What's wrong with Michelle?" Aerik asked.

"Mom thinks Michelle is a mean-girl name," Zoë replied.

"It *is* a mean-girl name!" I shot back.

"Mom, you're weird," Jackson said matter-of-factly.

That was the day the kids found out they had two moms. In the span of only a few minutes, they had expressed their feelings, supported one another, given her a new name, reaffirmed their love for our family and reminded us all how strange I am. I can't think of many other moments when I have been prouder to be their parent.

—

There were harder days over the next few weeks and months, of course. When a loved one transitions, a family transitions too. Part of that involves letting go of who you thought someone was and embracing who she is.

Early on, I described that process as something resembling grief. I no longer do. Many in the trans community have asked loved ones to reframe these emotions. Grief implies that the person is gone, after all, but they haven't died. They may look different, have a different name and use different pronouns, but they're still here—and often in better shape than before they came out. In this sense, mourning them seems excessive.

But letting go was a big part of the process for everyone after Zoë started her transition. I had to let go of the idea of having a husband and being in a heterosexual relationship. Our children had to let go of the idea of having a father, and the societal norm of living with opposite-sex parents.

Our biggest concern was that the kids would hide their feelings and pretend everything was fine so they wouldn't hurt their mama. Having already been through a loved one's transition, they knew it was a challenging time for the person transitioning. They might feel they were adding to Zoë's already full plate.

We made a point of checking in with them individually and as a group as often as possible. "We just want you to know it's okay to not be okay all the time," Zoë and I would remind them.

"I have my own feelings too," I once said to Jackson as he, Zoë and I sat on our queen-size bed. "Remember how much I cried in the first few weeks after Mama came out?"

"I thought you had cancer or something," Jackson said.

"Not cancer. Just a case of the sads," I replied.

"I felt sad at first too," he said. "Just a little. I thought I had a dad. I'm going to miss that."

Zoë nodded. "I'm sure you are, buddy."

"But I've been doing some thinking," Jackson continued. "And you know what's great about having two moms?"

"What's that?" Zoë and I asked in unison.

He reached over and hugged us both. "Everything."

—

Our entire family began the exhausting period of living two lives: the one we knew was true, and the one the rest of the world thought was true.

Because there was still so much to do before Zoë could present as herself full time, we needed to keep her identity private. This meant that inside the home, she was Zoë or Mama. Outside the home, everyone still knew her as her former self.

Zoë played a role all day at work, with a name and pronouns that didn't fit, then came home to dress and be referred to in a way that made her more comfortable. The daily switch was emotionally taxing. The more she embraced her true gender, the harder it was to pretend to be another, even if she had been doing it her entire life.

It was tough for the rest of us too. When we went out as a family, we had to be careful not to slip up with names or pronouns. The more internalized Zoë's womanhood and motherhood became to all of us, the less acceptable it felt to dishonour that by calling her "him" or "he" or "Dad." We became adept at gender-neutral language.

While doing my advocacy work, I referred to her as my spouse, my partner or my children's other parent. I also avoided using masculine pronouns whenever possible. If I couldn't refer to Zoë as her proper gender yet, I would do my best not to mis-gender her. The kids switched to using "parents" instead of "Mom and Dad." Even little Jackson switched over his language at school. He didn't have to—nobody asked him to or even sug-gested it—but he did it because it felt right.

It was time for Zoë to start telling the people closest to her. She called her parents in Peterborough to give them the news. She could have told them in person, but she chose the phone because she knew it would give them more space to react honestly without her in the room. She knew this wouldn't be easy, but her parents are kind and supportive people. They love their children and grandchildren, including the granddaughter they didn't know they had until she was eleven. Having some understanding of trans issues made it easier for them to hear and understand what Zoë was saying.

Still, they had thought Zoë was their eldest son. Finding out this wasn't true hit them hard. They immediately told her they loved her and supported her but would need some time to process it all. As a parent of a trans child myself, I understood this. When you've known your child for over forty years as someone of one gender, it takes time to adjust to a new reality. But they reiterated that they were 100 percent behind her.

When it came time to tell my parents about Zoë, it was different than telling them about Alexis. It meant answering questions about our relationship, and therefore questions about me.

"We hope to stay together," I said to them. "But if we break up, it's not because she's trans. Her being a woman isn't a deal-breaker."

In other words, Mom and Dad, I'm not straight.

I had known for a long time, but it was a fact I never thought I would have to reveal to my Catholic family members. I wasn't prepared to have a deep conversation with them about it, mostly because my sexual orientation had yet to be fully unpacked from the big box of shame I had kept it in my entire life.

Thankfully, that was the least of their concerns for the moment. Twenty-two years before, at the age of sixteen, I had brought Zoë to meet my parents for the first time. While we were there, we also mentioned that we had just moved in together. We continued to surprise them throughout our relationship, from unexpected pregnancies to staying together despite our chronic unhappiness. This was yet another surprise, a twist in a love story that was anything but typical.

My mom had questions and concerns she needed to discuss with us. She wanted to make sure that if we did stay together, we would end up in a better relationship on the other side of this transition; she knew how hard we had struggled for many years. Zoë assured her that she loved me deeply, and that all she wanted was to be able to love me as the woman she is. And I assured her that I loved my wife back, and that I believed, in time, we were going to be okay.

"Good," my mom said, being so very mom-like. "Because neither of you has been happy for years, and you both deserve that. You've been so standoffish the entire time I've known you, Zoë. Now I understand why. I look forward to getting to know you now." They hugged tightly in a way I had never seen before.

As we continued down the line with siblings, other extended family members and friends, our world became incrementally easier and safer. Unlike Alexis, Zoë came out gradually, like a slow bloom: first one petal, then another. It was months in the making, a dynamic experience in forging relationships in which we could all be ourselves.

A week or two after Zoë told the kids, we took Jackson camping with some of my food court girls and their families. We pitched our tents at a large pagan-focused festival most of them attended each year. I had gone the year before with Jackson and knew how inclusive it was. It was a place where Zoë could express herself in safety, even though there were hundreds of families on-site. The festival was welcoming to LGBTQ people. There was even an unofficial "rainbow camp" where many queer people grouped together, stringing colourful flags and other gay apparel all over their site. There were casual get-togethers and sacred rituals specifically for us, and even a small but popular pride parade through the campground.

Zoë shed all her masculine clothing while we were there. She donned a sarong most days and tied a colourful scarf around her short hair, which was slowly growing out. She went by the nickname Zo, which our friends used without question. She was in her element, and expressed to all of us how much better she felt living as herself full time. Even Jackson seemed relaxed now that he didn't have to play the pronoun game to get around outing his mama.

I, however, was struggling. Panic punched at my insides as I watched a person I'd known for two decades dress and behave in a completely different manner. It felt sudden and alien to me. The feminine clothing Zoë had started to wear at home was more gender-neutral in appearance. When I saw her in skirts, speaking in a higher pitch, her mannerisms more feminine than I was used to, I worried. It was a snapshot of where we were headed, and I wondered if people would be as kind beyond this festival. Would strangers laugh with her or at her? Would she be in danger? Would our kids be?

I should have been celebrating with her. Instead, I agonized over my family's future, filled once again with resentment over the curveball thrown our way. It wasn't fair. Why did this have to happen?

NINETEEN

stasis

THE WAITING GAME was eating Zoë alive—and so were the potential costs associated with transition. She was fortunate to have a workplace insurance plan that covered most of the cost of a private psychologist to do her initial assessment of gender dysphoria. That opened the door to medical treatments she needed much sooner than the six months it would take to get an appointment at the free clinic. We were both big believers in public health care, even if it meant slightly longer wait times for non-urgent issues. However, time is not on a trans person's side if medical transition is needed. Long wait times have been shown to cause depression and increase suicide rates.

And Zoë was struggling to get through each day. She hated her body, her voice, every reflection, every phone call. She flinched when people called her sir. The pain of dealing with the outside world made her sad and frustrated. These emotions turned to anger, fuelled in part by the unwanted testosterone still surging through her body. She knew she was quick to get angry, quick to push those closest to her away—a fallback to a time when keeping her distance meant keeping her secret safe.

She knew I wanted to be there for her, wanted to help, but I didn't know how. "There's nothing you can do," Zoë would say. "I just need these appointments to start happening. I needed this yesterday. I needed it years ago."

Locked in stasis. Waiting. It was torture.

It would take one thing to ruin her day, and I never knew what that one thing would be. In public, my guard would go up. I overcompensated, trying to do all the talking and protect her from conversations where she might get misgendered. When she came home from work, thoroughly exhausted from having played White Collar Man all day, I would try to make things as easy as I could: dinner ready, house clean, any child-related issues already dealt with. Because that was all I could offer. I had read up on how to support someone through dysphoria and realized that all I could do was cheer her on or comfort her, depending on what she needed that day.

This profound feeling of distress was one I would never fully understand. The closest I came was back when I was heavier, and people would sometimes assume I was pregnant. A few even ran up and touched my belly excitedly. It was a reminder of how big I was, how uncomfortable and sore within my body, and how melancholy this made me. Still, my womanhood had never been called into question. When people assumed Zoë was a man, it was a reminder of how the world saw her, and how at odds that was with how she felt inside. This cut to the core of her identity.

On the really bad days, I would sit next to her in bed while she curled up in that familiar fetal position, not wanting to leave the safety of the covers.

"I'm so ugly," she would say.

"You're not ugly," I would reply. "You're beautiful."

"I look like a guy," she would say.

"Things are going to get better, okay? It just takes time."

A few weeks after that fateful conversation in the car, she was able to see a gender identity therapist, and she diagnosed Zoë's case as "classic." This was a good thing, since it meant there would be no extra delay. After a few sessions, she referred Zoë to the endocrinologist who would start her on the right medical path.

Meanwhile, there were things that weren't covered by either public or private insurance, like laser and electrolysis treatments to remove her facial hair. Those treatments cost thousands of dollars—by far the biggest out-of-pocket expense we incurred. Both the government and the insurance company deemed the procedures to be cosmetic. Many trans women would argue they're essential.

Throughout those early days, Zoë showed amazing resiliency. She was still a very committed parent, still excelled at her demanding job and still held on through the bumps of us rebuilding our relationship from the ground up. I had thought I was the strong one in our marriage. I take it back.

But we had a long road ahead. Even with the fast-tracked timeline, she couldn't live as herself full time until spring of 2016, half a year away. During that period, she would see the psychologist and the endocrinologist, continue with hair removal and change her ID. It was a sensible timeline, but it meant months longer in the closet for all of us.

All the while, I was blogging about my family's continuing journey through Alexis's transition, giving public talks (sometimes with our daughter), working with media and using social media as an advocacy platform. It was a juggling act to do all this while also keeping Zoë's gender identity a secret—and I'm a terrible juggler.

In the late summer of 2015, just weeks after Zoë came out, I got an email from Microsoft Canada's marketing team. The company wanted Alexis and me to be part of a campaign to promote using technology to create positive change. It was to be called #My24hrs and would feature activists and changemakers from across the country. Microsoft had a keen interest in featuring us—trans kids were at the forefront of a new fight for inclusion and equality, and we were a family working to spread that message.

The plan was simple: we would travel to Toronto to do an in-studio interview, and that interview, coupled with footage that would be shot later in Ottawa, would be turned into a video explaining our advocacy work and how we were using blogging and social media to create change in the world.

I knew this could be a game changer. With a giant like Microsoft backing us, we could reach a whole new audience. The company's support would lend significant weight to our message of embracing trans youth for who they are. I could imagine a young trans person watching the video and feeling hopeful because one of the world's most prominent companies was supporting them. What would have happened if Alexis had seen something like that earlier in her life?

But I also knew that the increased exposure associated with this campaign carried risk. Would my children become targets for more hate? Would they be applauded at school for their candour or taunted for taking such a strong stand? It was impossible to tell.

I worried about being able to handle such a public project. Would I be riddled with such anxiety that there weren't enough crullers in the world to manage it? I knew I would question myself at every step, convinced that I was way out of my league and the Microsoft people would soon realize they had gambled on the wrong woman.

I even worried about Microsoft. Yes, that's right. At times like these, I am the mom to everyone, including forward-thinking, multi-billion-dollar companies. But the backlash could be significant: angry customers, vicious comments and even boycotts were possible. This was right around the time when Target merged their boys' and girls' toys and Cheerios began featuring ads with same-sex parents. The pushback from a subset of consumers with highly conservative "values" was loud and intense. What would happen if a giant tech company promoted a family accepting a trans child?

But mostly, I worried about Zoë, who was at a vulnerable juncture in her life. She had only recently disclosed her news to a select group of people, and she wasn't ready to be out to the world yet—much less part of a video campaign. To most people, she was still Alexis's dad. On the other hand, representing herself as Alexis's dad in that campaign wouldn't be right either. The timing of this offer couldn't have been worse.

I called my wife, pacing the bedroom with a knot in my stomach. She was at work and answered in a deeper voice than she'd been using at home. It threw me for a second.

"Hey," I said. "I just got off the phone with someone at Microsoft. They want to work with us."

"*The* Microsoft?" she asked, sounding as surprised as I felt.

"No, the other one," I replied sarcastically.

I explained how they wanted to profile our family. "It's an amazing opportunity," I said. "This could be significant in the fight to support trans kids."

"No kidding," Zoë replied. I could almost hear her trying to take in the scope of it.

"But the thing is, I think they want the whole family involved."

"Oh," she replied, worry creeping into her voice. She had arrived at the same place where I was, sitting on the fence between excitement and panic. Great opportunity, terrible timing.

"I know what you're thinking," I said. "Don't worry, I haven't agreed to anything. I haven't even talked to Alexis because I wanted to see how you felt about it first. Your safety and comfort are my top priority right now."

"No, the priority is to help kids like Alexis," she said immediately. "I don't want them to end up like me, having to do this in their forties. It's awful. Let's figure out how to do this right, okay?"

It was decided: Zoë was one extraordinary woman.

I told the people at Microsoft that we would love to take part, but my spouse couldn't participate too heavily. They were fine with that. They wanted to focus on Alexis and me—and while any other family members who wished to take part were welcome, there would be no pressure. I didn't tell them why Zoë couldn't participate because it didn't matter. They were capturing our family the way it looked at that point in time, and if it happened to look different a few months after the campaign was over, so be it. Families change all the time—just not always in this way.

In October, Zoë, Alexis and I drove to Toronto to film the in-studio interview part of our video. Alexis and I had our makeup and hair done, then sat on a couch in front of bright lights to answer questions about her journey so far and what it meant to our family. It was an unforgettable experience.

Afterward, Zoë took Alexis home to Ottawa so I could head directly to an event north of Toronto to speak on stage for the first time. Blissdom Canada was a yearly social media conference covering topics from growing an audience to working with companies. The world had changed in the nine years since I had started blogging. What used to be a hobby for a few of us was now a career for thousands. And it wasn't just blogging anymore; there were videos, Twitter parties (where everyone uses the same hashtag to promote the issue or business they're talking about) and carefully staged Instagram or Pinterest photos. This was all part of "building your brand."

I knew nothing about building my brand. My "brand"—if I chose to call it that—was to write blog posts and share them on social media. I didn't monetize my site, and I didn't make special efforts to grow followers on any platform. I just wrote for the love of it. Some people read my posts and shared them, and my audience grew organically. By all accounts, this made me a social media dinosaur.

But I wasn't asked to be a part of this conference for my branding prowess. The organizers wanted to showcase people who used their platform to make a difference in the world—a topic in which I had growing experience. I would share the stage with other women who were fighting for their own causes. One had been sexually assaulted and chose to speak publicly about it, while another was a Muslim woman working to dispel misconceptions surrounding her faith. Our common bond was that all of us had found ourselves faced with injustice and refused to stay quiet. It sounded as if it could be a fruitful discussion.

A shame about all the freaking out I was doing, though.

I wondered what I could possibly add to the conversation. Would I have anything insightful to say, or would I freeze up? I also didn't know how big the audience would be or whether people would be receptive to my message. As I knew all too well, not everyone believes in affirming trans kids. Some even consider it a form of child abuse. If I were in the audience, would I want to hear from someone I thought was a child abuser? Probably not.

And in the back of mind, but always in the centre of my heart, was Zoë. I had to make sure not to out her. I needed to be careful at this conference full of people with large social media followings not to disclose anything I shouldn't.

But no pressure, Amanda.

The panel was being held the next day. There were several small breakout rooms where workshops were held, but I couldn't find where ours would be.

"That's because you're going to be presenting right here," one of the organizers explained.

'Right here' was a large, beautifully decorated reception room with a big stage where the keynote speakers would be doing their thing.

"Oh," I replied, trying not to follow it up with "shit."

"We were going to make it a workshop, but there's been a lot of interest, so we're going big."

"Great!" I replied cheerily, wondering where the nearest bathroom was so I could go throw up in it.

I couldn't find a nearby bathroom, so I made a beeline to my hotel room. It was large, sunny and had a lovely view of the mountains, which calmed me down significantly. But most importantly, it was all mine. In nearly forty years, I had never had my own hotel room, and I didn't know where to start. Should I roll around on the bed, strut around the room naked like a boss or live-tweet myself eating room service in my underwear? There were too many fantastic options to choose from.

I opted to enjoy the quiet for a moment and take stock of where I was.

For a long time, I had been a mom and budding writer with no steady career outside the home and little job experience. I had mostly kept to my same group of friends and daily routines, with only a blog as evidence to the world that I existed. I had striven to blend in with everyone because it offered the least amount of risk of rejection.

But now, seemingly overnight, I had a message, a growing audience and new opportunities to share our family's journey. I was now an advocate, someone people looked to for guidance on a subject still vastly misunderstood. I had never expected this to happen and I felt ill-equipped to manage it. Inside, I was still that lonely girl in the schoolyard, still the teen who was set on fire. I was still the woman who wondered how she could fit in when she felt so out of place. I was still the one whose father had never bothered to get to know her.

I had become friendly with some other attendees since I arrived at the conference. But would they be as friendly once I stepped off that stage tomorrow? What about at the next conference, when the world knew more about my family than I was disclosing now? Would they unfriend me on Facebook as quickly as they'd added me? Between working with Microsoft and gearing up to speak in front of my first large audience, I was feeling the glare of the spotlight a little too intensely.

I ate nothing the next morning. I couldn't eat, for fear of

throwing up on my cute little blazer. My only sustenance for several hours was coffee, which is the wrong thing to consume when you're excruciatingly nervous. I began to think I couldn't do this. I was a writer, not a public speaker. I'd picked writing as a career because it allowed me time to formulate my thoughts before putting them out there. (Also, I don't have to wear pants.)

I had given a few radio interviews, but even when done live, they didn't happen on a large stage in front of hundreds of people, with lights and microphones and the potential for booing. In fact, they were usually done on my cellphone in the basement as I sat on the old stained couch in the dark. (Pants optional.)

But before I knew it—and well before I was ready—it was time. I was ushered to the front of the room, next to the stage. I stood beside the other people who would be appearing with me. I was relieved to see I wasn't the only nervous one.

We were introduced one a time. When I was called up, I heard encouraging cheers from the crowd and held on tightly to that positivity as I made my way up the stairs. I waved awkwardly to the crowd, partially blinded by the bright spotlights, and then settled in for what ended up being an empowering discussion.

I spoke about leading with love and letting everything else fall into place. I spoke about the thorny path of advocacy, but said I would walk it until the day I died for my child. As I spoke, the giant screens on each side of the stage showed one of my recent tweets: "I used to not want to rock the boat, but I think I tipped it over a long time ago and am now using it as a battering ram."

Mostly, I remember how I felt both during and afterward. Speaking is like writing on steroids. It has all the benefits of connecting with an audience, but in an instantaneous and dynamic way. Not sure if you're getting your message across? Just have a look into the crowd. Are people watching intently? Are they nodding in agreement? Are they clapping when you say some-thing important? If not, switch up how you connect with them. Check in with them. Ask them a question, provide more of what they need.

Writing, for all its beauty, is a one-shot deal. You have all the time you need to formulate a thought, but once you publish it, it's done. You've either hit the target or you've missed. Your words either reach the desired audience or they don't.

Speaking, in many ways, is an extension of writing. It com-plements the work I do, and despite the initial stress, I found it exceptionally rewarding.

Afterward, people lined up to talk to me. One woman hung back until the crowd dissipated. When she did speak, she began to cry. She told me she thought one of her children might be trans and I was the first person she had met who could under-stand her mix of feelings. It was the first time I met in person someone who was directly impacted by our story. We talked, hugged and exchanged information. We're still in touch today.

The power of personal connection is beyond compare. I've spoken many times since then, on stages across the country, and I've loved each opportunity to meet the people our story reaches.

But you never forget your first.

TWENTY

insidious

IN DECEMBER 2015, some friends invited me to see *The Danish Girl*, the story of a transgender woman and her wife in 1920s Copenhagen.

If you ask many members of the transgender community, they'll tell you the movie is problematic. For one thing, while it's based on a true story, it's not historically accurate. Also, the film focuses a great deal on the internal suffering of the trans character, which is a one-dimensional view of trans experiences. There is also the chronic Hollywood issue of having a cisgender person play a transgender character, even though there are plenty of talented trans actors in the industry. I don't disagree with any of this.

However, I will say that the movie played a key role in solidifying my marriage. The plot centres around Lili, a closeted trans woman born in a time when most people did not understand the complexities of gender. When presenting as male becomes unbearable, Lili comes out to her wife, Gerda, and together they start seeking answers to Lili's internal struggle.

I found myself lost in the story and relating heavily to what Gerda was experiencing. Her fierce protection of and fears for her wife were tangible to me. Lili's struggles, meanwhile, reminded me so much of Zoë's. I could see how hard she tried to hide. I could see she had no choice but to be herself at all costs. I saw this movie at just the right time for it all to have a profound impact on my life.

I came home and broke into tears in the kitchen.

"What's wrong?" Zoë asked, concern forming on her face.

"Oh, honey," I said, putting my arms around her and burying my gross wet face in her neck.

"Are you okay?" she asked. "Did something happen?"

"Yes!" I said, scanning the counter for therapy cookies. There were none. Bloody hell.

"What happened?" she asked, holding me closer.

"It was the stupid movie!" I cried.

"The movie? *The Danish Girl* one?"

"Oh my God, I get it now. I get it!"

"What do you mean?" she asked.

"It was our story! Except like a hundred years ago, and in Europe, and they were artists and had no kids!"

"So . . . *not* our story," she corrected.

I pulled away and wiped my tears on my sleeve. "No, not our story *exactly*," I said, giving her a teary red eye-roll. "But the trans woman was hurting and just trying to be herself, and her wife was hurting and trying to be supportive. And it was so sad and beautiful. It was basically us, but younger and with nicer lipstick. Do we have cookies?"

"I love you," she said, laughing.

I took her by the shoulders and looked her in the eye to make sure that she heard every word I was about to say. "I want you to know I'm in this for the long haul. We're in this together, okay?"

She looked surprised. "You don't have to say that, you know. You can take more time."

"I've taken all the time I need."

I meant it. It was time to rebuild that demolished foundation of ours.

<hr />

We were all doing our best to get through the final closeted months. Zoë was preparing to be physically and legally out full time. She had quietly spoken with her boss, her closest co-workers and the human resources people. They said she was the first person they knew of to transition within the company. They vowed to make sure that the Ontario Human Rights Code was followed to the letter, and that Zoë was treated with dignity and respect. When the time came, she would give them a heads-up so they could take the final steps needed for her to transition on the job.

But for now, we waited. Half in the closet, half out.

And while we waited, Microsoft came to film the B-roll, or background footage, for our video. Zoë is in exactly one shot in the final product, and only the back of her head is visible. The rest of it is mostly of me and Alexis, along with some clips from Alexis's middle school principal talking about the importance of inclusion in education, and a visit to Kind Space, a local LGBTQ organization to which Microsoft donated in our name. The video was released in late February 2016, and we were proud of it.

Overall, the reception was positive, but I watched some negative comments scroll by on my Twitter feed, and a few pieces of hate mail landed in my inbox. I wondered if Microsoft would be hit with a boycott, as had happened to other companies that stood up for LGBTQ rights. I was relieved not to see one. More importantly, I started hearing from other families like ours, with kids like our own, who were grateful to see such a large company openly support them. Visibility truly does make a difference.

Zoë was building up her wardrobe and getting bolder with what she wore at work. She was exclusively dressing in clothes from the women's department, but she chose to wear the more gender-neutral pieces to the office.

"Aren't you worried someone is going to notice, though?" I asked her one morning as she was getting ready.

"What if they do? What are they going to say?" she replied. "'Hey, are you wearing women's jeans?' I don't think anyone is going to ask that. And if they do, I'll just say I am and watch them try to follow that up in a work-appropriate way."

I laughed at the thought.

"Besides," she continued, "here's the thing about most people: they see the world as they want to see it."

"What do you mean?"

"People tend to put others into a box. Right now, everyone sees me as male. So unless I wear something very obviously feminine that throws that into question, they're going to assume I'm a man wearing men's clothing."

I thought back to all the times when there had been signs of Zoë's true gender, and how I had assumed they were signs of something else: a man being uncomfortable with his body, a man not fitting in with other men, a man trying to bond with his children. All reasonable assumptions, for sure, but assumptions based on the binary box in which my mind had always placed her.

She was right. She went to work every day in these clothes and was never once questioned or given a strange look. When she started to let her closest co-workers know about her transition, I wondered if the light came on for them as it had for me when I finally put all the pieces together.

―

Winter is particularly harsh in Ottawa. We're the snowiest capital city in the world, with an average of 224 centimetres, or 88 inches, of snowfall each year. Temperatures can dip deep into the negatives and stay that way for days at a time. You might see your neighbours a couple of times in December and not again until April, when we all emerge from near hibernation, groggy and grateful for warmer weather. It's not a fun few months for the happiest of people. But when you're feeling overloaded by life, our northern climate, with its dark days and isolation, can make things even worse.

I chronically shelve my feelings and remind myself that other people have it worse. I've been doing this for most of my life: using empathy for others as a reason to push my own emotions aside. "It's not that bad," I'll tell myself. "Just look at what So-and-so is going through. Suck it up, Amanda. In comparison, you're fine."

In this case, So-and-so's name was Zoë, and I knew she was dealing with an inordinate amount of stress while leading essentially two lives. Sure, I had stress too. But it was nothing compared to hers, right?

I knew Alexis was also dealing with her own stresses, including trying to be a typical grade eight girl when your body is in a medically induced pubescent stasis. She wouldn't get the green light for hormones from the gender-identity clinic until at least her fourteenth birthday, which was still months away. Meanwhile, she watched as her classmates grew curves and breasts, looking more and more like she had always wanted to. "But lots of girls start developing later," people who meant well would tell her. That doesn't matter, though, when you're waiting for a doctor's approval rather than a flood of hormones. She was at the mercy of other people's understanding.

Then there were our boys, quietly putting the pieces of their lives back together in a way that made sense to them. For the most part, they appeared strong and together, but I had a feeling there was more going on beneath the surface.

Aerik was in his first year of college after a challenging final year of high school. He had blamed a lot of his grade twelve stresses on having too much schoolwork, but I wondered if his problems were linked to the changes at home. Now he was doing well and making new friends, but I could see him trying to balance his more independent adult life with his need to be present for his younger siblings.

Jackson, meanwhile, was having trouble concentrating at school. While we suspected ADHD, the psychologist advised us to hold off on getting him assessed. "He's been through so many changes that there's no way to make a definitive diagnosis right now," he explained. So until the dust settled, our youngest would continue getting distracted in school, getting in trouble for disrupting the class and getting picked on by his peers because of it.

Everyone was going through big things, and I needed to be

there for them. My own little box of feels sat high on a shelf, and whenever it looked like it was going to pop open, I would just put something heavy on top and say, "I'll deal with this later."

Let me explain what happens when I deal with things "later."

Buying our home in 2013 was an absolute nightmare. We were moving from one province to another, and that required different paperwork than anyone realized, additional lawyer's fees and a last-minute loan reapplication. We were handed signed papers at the bank just minutes before they were due to be notarized in another building. Then we had a surprise bad home inspection on the house we were selling, and that resulted in a significant price drop from our buyers and a move we couldn't afford unless we did it entirely ourselves. It became a panic buffet with a heaping side of freak out.

Except I didn't panic. I didn't freak out. I held it together because *I didn't have time for that.* We had a home to sell and another to move into. We had kids who needed a roof over their heads. I shelved my stress in an ever-growing box with a bunch of heavy stuff piled on top. Later. I would deal with it later.

Everything eventually came together. The night we moved in, I told myself it was all worth it—the stress was finally behind us, and I could relax in the recliner I had just set up in the family room. As soon as I sat in the chair and turned on the TV, I felt an irregular thump in my chest, followed by a couple more. This didn't stop. The next day, I was at the walk-in clinic. For the following three days, I wore a heart monitor. The irregular thumping didn't stop for about two weeks.

Thankfully, the heart palpitations turned out to be a harmless physical reaction to stress. But they did tell me something important: I am the type of person who, when she refuses to deal with the feelings in front of her, will have to deal with them blowing up in her face (or in her chest) at a later time.

I've also learned I'm the type of person who usually needs to learn a lesson more than once.

One weekday morning, I was sitting in my favourite breakfast place with my grown-up schoolyard friend Allison, the parent council chair. We used to meet about once a week and order the exact same breakfast special: two eggs over easy, sausages and rye toast. We were predictable and our server loved us for it. She had stopped bringing us menus months before.

"You know," I said that day to Allison, "I've been feeling a little off lately. I don't know what's wrong."

"Well, there's a lot going on right now," she said. She was one of the first people I'd told about Zoë. I had sat on her steps one evening and cried uncontrollably. She had never seen me so upset. Now, sitting across the table from her a few months after my breakdown, I spoke in a level tone about some thoughts I'd been having.

"To be honest, I've thought about dying a few times."

"Oh, yeah?" Allison replied, in her best keep-it-cool voice.

"I mean, I'm not going to do it," I said. "I have kids who need me. But I want to die sometimes because everything is so hard right now. It would be a relief, frankly."

Allison put down her fork.

"Um," she began, as delicately as she could, "I think maybe you should talk to your doctor."

"Yeah?" I took a sip of coffee and glanced at the paintings lining the walls. I used to paint all the time, but I hadn't picked up a brush in months. "Maybe."

"Why don't you see if you can make an appointment?"

"Okay. I'll do that." I wasn't going to do that.

"No, like right now. Give them a call. Maybe they can squeeze you in today. You never know."

"I doubt that, but okay," I said. I started searching for the number on my phone, not quite understanding why she was insisting that I call the doctor. Miraculously, someone answered the phone at the exceptionally busy clinic. Even more miraculously, the doctor could see me that afternoon. Two exceptions to the rule that had never happened before and have not happened since.

I often think about that day, and whether I would have called the doctor at all if Allison hadn't insisted. What if they hadn't answered? Would I have bothered to leave a message or call back later? What if the doctor hadn't been able to see me? Would I have gone to an appointment a few days from then? I'm going to guess no on all accounts.

I was in such denial, so unaware of how sick I was, that the fantasies about killing myself seemed entirely natural. Even though I had been depressed before and knew what that felt like, this had come on so quietly, so insidiously, that I hadn't noticed until I was suffocated by it. I didn't realize I was no longer finding joy in the things I loved doing—if I even bothered doing them at all.

I believe I didn't see what was happening partly because I was so good at self-care by this point. I ate well, slept well, exercised regularly and even had a therapist. How could I possibly be depressed if I was doing all the right things? But even as I left the restaurant and made my way home before my appointment, the veil that depression had carefully placed over my eyes was falling away.

By the time I got to the doctor's office, I was ready to talk. Because he was also Zoë's doctor, what I told him about our family wasn't a surprise. I explained how everything had gone grey in the past few months, and how I couldn't seem to find my way out of it. I told him I had no set plan to die, but I wouldn't be opposed to it either. I said that when I drove my car alone, I often thought about going really fast and hitting something really hard—I just never went through with it.

We completed a depression checklist and I scored high in symptoms. We did an anxiety checklist and I scored even higher. I started to cry, telling him how frustrated this made me. I had taken charge of my health and was prioritizing it, despite having many excuses at the ready. He told me that our brains sometimes need help anyway, and that if I was willing to try an antidepressant, I would likely see improvement. It could get me over this hump.

I left with a prescription I was hesitant to fill. The paper felt like failure in my hands. This is what mental illness can do: it can rob us of healthy perspective and fill us with shame. *I'm not strong enough. I'm not good enough.* Never in a million years would I say those things to someone I loved who was depressed. I would say, "Take the damn meds if you need them." I would encourage them, check up on them and love them through it. Yet when the shoe was on the other foot, I was filled with berating thoughts.

I took the damn meds anyway.

You know when things have been cloudy for days on end and you think the sun is never going to come out again, but then it does? About three weeks after I slinked out of the doctor's office with that prescription, the sun came out and it was beautiful. It's not that the problems were no longer there—it's that they were more manageable. Instead of feeling overwhelmed by them, I could give each one attention and then put it away for a while to deal with something else. I didn't have to think about Zoë's transition 24/7. I could tell myself we were doing everything we could to help Jackson right now and believe it. I knew that Aerik would be fine; at nineteen, he was an adult with good communication skills and could come to us if he had issues he couldn't manage. And Alexis had an abundance of support to get her through this time in stasis until she could start her hormone therapy. She would be okay too. They all would be.

And you know who else was going to be okay? Me. I felt it to the bone. It was the sweet relief I hadn't realized I needed.

Manageability in the midst of change. Finally.

TWENTY-ONE

daylight

ZOË'S BIRTHDAY was at the end of January, and she hadn't had a party in a very long time.

To be fair, Zoë, in her previous societal role, was not that interested in parties. She preferred solitude. But now? The girl was all about celebrating her birthday. And the growing number of friends and family members she had come out to were eager to celebrate with her. I decided to plan a "Zoë's first birthday" event.

We don't live in a large home. So when I invited two dozen people over, I did it expecting only half of them to show up.

I am not a good estimator.

Everyone showed up. The house was packed with people, including Zoë's parents, my mom, one of Zoë's co-workers and a large number of female friends. They brought her thoughtful gifts like an engraved jewellery box with her name and birthday on it. Her mom surprised her with her late grandmother's ring, which made just about everyone cry. As I watched my wife, surrounded by a circle of other women, sharing in stories and laughter, I remembered that party all those years ago, when she had stood on the outside of the circle looking in. Seeing her now, it was clear she was in her element at last. This is where she belonged, had always belonged, and she was finally here.

Our eyes met across the room. "I love you," she mouthed.

"I love you too," I mouthed back. My heart beat a little faster in my chest. It wasn't palpitations this time.

Zoë was now months into her medical transition and was eagerly awaiting the changes to her birth certificate and other identification. She had told family, good friends and those she worked most closely with at the office, but we both realized it was time to start telling the other people in our personal lives. We decided a friends-only post on Facebook was the fastest and easiest way to do this. I would post it, since Zoë had deleted her old account and had yet to create a fresh one under her new name.

At the time, the people on my Facebook list were those we knew in person, fellow parents of trans children and some I had met online through my blog or our recent media exposure. All of them were LGBTQ community members or allies. (Everyone else had weeded themselves out after we told them about Alexis.) In theory, this meant that every person who was about to find out the news would be good with it.

Still, I worried—not only about bigotry but also about loose talk. Would someone take a screenshot and share it? Would I get calls from a local reporter looking for a follow-up story on the family with the trans child who, it was now rumoured, also had a transitioning parent? Would Zoë's co-workers who didn't yet know get wind of this too soon? And if so, what would be the consequences?

There are times when queer people are chastised for not "coming out right."

"Why did you wait so long?"

"Why did you tell us in a letter?"

"Why did you write a public post before letting your family know? Are we not important?"

"Why did you have to announce it at all? It's nobody's business. Just live your life."

"Why didn't you say something before surprising us with it? You just showed up to dinner with your boyfriend and that's how we find out?"

No matter how we do it, people judge us for it. But what they often don't understand is how messy, complicated and utterly exhausting it can be to come out. Society's default is straight. Society's other default is cisgender. People generally assume you're both unless you tell them otherwise. As a result, those of us who don't fit into those categories end up coming out to people, over and over, for the rest of our lives.

When we do say something about who we are or who we love, we do it in the best way we can, with whatever energy we can give to it and in the way that is safest. We take many things into consideration, but ultimately this declaration needs to serve our own interests. We owe it to ourselves to do it in a way that feels right, and we hope the people who love us will understand that.

In this case, the people who love us did a bang-up job of showing it. When I wrote that Facebook post, it was a coming out for both of us. "Hey, everyone! Zoë is a woman. I am not straight. Check out this stick of dynamite we're using to blow up our walk-in closet!" (That's not exactly what I wrote, but I should have.)

We told everyone who Zoë was and what this meant for our

family. I said that I was more in love with her than ever, and that the kids were happy to have two moms. I asked for their support and kindness but offered the same "out" as I had when we told everyone about Alexis: if you can't be on board, please quietly exit our lives.

Finally, I made a plea for privacy.

Yes, we asked hundreds of people to keep this news quiet for two or three more weeks until Zoë came out at work and I had figured out a plan to deal with what I knew would be a media frenzy. It was a big ask.

But they came through. Every single one of them. They cheered for Zoë, sent countless messages of support our way and waited for my wife to tell the rest of the world in her own time. They created a safe place online by forming a protective wall around our family.

From friends to family to neighbours to co-workers, we have people of the highest calibre in our corner.

—

A few days later, Zoë got the official documentation with her new name and gender marker. She was now Zoë Michelle Knox, and her birth certificate had an "F" on it instead of an "M."

She was thrilled to see her name in print. I was two-thirds thrilled, because I was understandably still hung up on the whole Michelle thing. The good news was I had recently met a Michelle I liked, and I believed, through her, I could learn to overcome my prejudice.

We stared at Zoë's shiny new birth certificate with amazement. It had taken letters from doctors, a pile of forms and some money thrown the government's way to make this happen. But with this, we had finally come to the end of a long stay in the closet.

"That's it," Zoë told me, letting out a relieved sigh. "That was the last thing I needed to make it happen. They can change my name in the company system, make me a new badge and I'm good to go. Can you believe it?"

"No, I can't," I replied. "I also can't believe I have a wife named Michelle."

She stuck out her tongue.

It was time for Zoë to set an official coming-out date. She chose Friday, March 11, 2016, and gave HR a heads-up. Our family of five collectively got ready for what was to come. There was no doubt things were going to change with Zoë finally able to live as Zoë. On the plus side, we wouldn't have to hide any longer. No need to remember who knows and who doesn't, or to carefully navigate around pronouns. Jackson, Alexis and Aerik could finally tell anyone they chose that they have two moms, and I could tell the world I have a wife.

But there were some potential negatives too. Zoë could be a target for bigotry. The kids could face anything from uncomfortable questions to outright discrimination. Our family could be harassed in public. I also knew the media would have a field day with this story, and I was trying to figure out how to shield us from the wrong coverage. For all the good I knew we had done, this was one time I wished we hadn't been so public with Alexis's story.

We expected some curiosity, questions, ignorance and even hatred from the outside world—we just weren't sure how much. Most of this was out of our control, however, so we tried to focus on what we could control, like building up my wife's wardrobe.

My friend Annie gave Zoë two big bags of work clothes. Annie is a tall woman with great style. With these new items and what Zoë had already picked out for herself at the store, her side of the closet was looking fab. We don't have the same body type or shoe size, but I did make a play for sharing scarves, purses and jewellery. She reluctantly agreed.

My wife is very organized in a way that I, as a chaotic artist type, envy. She had a notebook with a checklist of things that needed to happen before she could live as herself full time: medical, legal and social. She had diligently worked through these items over the past few months, crossing them off as she went. I probably would have asked Siri to make memos on the fly, and then accidentally deleted the memos, and then just cried in bed with the dog because I didn't know what to do next.

With this birth certificate, every item in her notebook list had been crossed off except the very last one: come out at work.

"Are you ready to be out to the world?" I asked on her last night in the closet.

"I think so," she replied nervously.

I held her hand. "This is the start of a whole new life. I'm so proud of you." What it took for her to get here was nothing short of inspiring. It was impossible not to love this woman.

Neither of us slept much that night. When I did manage a few winks, anxiety filled my dreams.

—

On March 11, 2016, Zoë, the girl from Peterborough who ran far and fast for way too long, sent an email to hundreds of her work colleagues. In it, she told them she was transgender. She explained she had always known she was a woman and was finally taking steps to live as one. She reminded them she was the same person with the same skill set and abilities she'd always had, and asked for their continued respect. She said she was going to take a week off so that her name could be changed in the system and people could have a few days to process what she had just told them. When she came back, she said, she would look quite different, and she asked her co-workers to please use her new name and pronouns. She then closed the laptop, pushed it away and went down to the family room to panic silently under the guise of watching TV.

It was done and there was no going back. Never again would she have to pretend to be *him*. No matter what happened, from this moment on, the girl from Peterborough was finally free.

At the same time, I was doing my own form of silent panicking. I had a blog post ready to go right after Zoë sent her "It's a girl!" email announcement. In the spirit of the one I wrote about Alexis, it was entitled "World, Meet My Wife." I opened with our talk in the car, spoke in general terms about how challenging things had been over the past eight months and explained that we had now come to a good place in our relationship, that our family was happy and that Zoë was coming out at work that day.

"This is the internet," I observed, "so I expect not all of you will be supportive. But believe me, there isn't a thing you could say in response to this news that I haven't already thought of in the last several months. I used to worry about the shade people would throw our way, but not anymore. Our world is so full of love and support that it leaves absolutely no room for hatred or ignorance to reside within it."

This was entirely true. Another truth was that I had been building up one hell of a backbone. After two years of defending our child and helping her carve out safe places for herself, I finally knew how to manage haters. As the family member with the biggest online presence, I was the one bigots usually sought out to say awful things to. Unfortunately for them, I had become far less generous with my time and energy.

"Besides," I continued, "on top of having both a transgender daughter and wife, I've been fully immersed in gender issues for two years now, studying research, interviewing experts, giving talks, writing articles, and connecting with thousands of families. So unless you're coming at this with at least as much knowledge as I have now, I'm probably not going to pay your negativity much mind. Just sayin'."

After nearly four decades, I was done with bullies and wanted to make that abundantly clear.

Once Zoë had pressed Send on her email, I pressed Publish on my post. I then joined her downstairs to "watch TV," which meant staring at it and not processing a damn thing on the screen.

"Have you checked your email since you sent it?" I asked her as we gazed at the flashy pictures on the wall rectangle.

"Nope. Have you checked your blog?"

"Nope."

"Cool."

We stayed like that for a while, away from the internet. I worried people would say awful things about our family and about Zoë herself, and I wouldn't be able to protect us from it. Her worry was that no one would reply to her email. No one would say anything mean, of course, as that could get them in trouble with HR. But some might choose not to respond, not to show any support at all, and she wouldn't know why. She would then have to return to work without knowing what awaited her there.

But right now, our lives were like Schrödinger's cat, both alive and dead at the same time. We didn't know how the internet or her colleagues were reacting because we hadn't peeked. Until we did, we were both supported *and* unsupported by everyone.

The rectangular wall box kept showing moving pictures and we kept watching it in a zombie-like state. I wanted to stay just like that forever.

Eventually, Zoë went upstairs and grabbed her laptop.

"Holy cow," she said, looking at her screen. "I think I'm okay."

Within minutes of sending her email, she had received dozens of replies, and they just kept coming in. All of them were kind and respectful, and many were outright congratulatory. One of the first was from a VP who adamantly stated his support for her. A few colleagues commended her for taking this step, and some said the respect they already had for her had only grown with this news.

Zoë was still glad she had scheduled a week off to let any water-cooler talk die down. It would take a while for things to return to normal, but the responses were putting some of her fears to rest.

Now it was my turn. I pulled myself away from the TV and hesitantly grabbed my phone from the table. It was lighting up constantly with notifications from Facebook and Twitter. My blog post was being shared widely, and the comments were nearly all positive. My inbox was filling up with messages congratulating Zoë and commending our family for leading with love.

Of course, there were haters too, and they would come out to play in larger numbers over the next couple of weeks. But from that day on, we were a couple of out and proud wives in a family with two trans people. This was our reality. No more hiding. To the girl who'd never wanted to draw attention to herself and never wanted to rock the boat, this felt like freedom.

I was at the top of the mountain, proudly holding a flag and my wife's hand. Life changes you.

TWENTY-TWO

reaction

IT WAS MONDAY, and the girl from Peterborough was going back to work.

"Are you nervous?" I asked.

"Of course," she replied.

"Yeah, stupid question." We both smiled faintly.

Despite the warm email response, she wondered if she would be greeted with as much kindness in person. Would people be whispering just beyond earshot? Would they avoid her? Be awkward around her? There was no way to know until she walked through the company doors.

"Do you want me to come with you?" I asked. "I mean it. I'm happy to walk you right to your desk. I'll slap my advocacy pants on right now!"

Zoë loved me, that much I knew. In the past two years, she had watched me morph into a stronger, more confident person. She had seen me overcome a lot of my own demons to be the mom, partner and advocate I wanted to be. But Zoë also worried about being viewed as someone to be taken care of. She didn't need anyone to do that. She was stronger than ever too.

"I'll be fine," she reassured me.

"Okay, but you had better text me and let me know how things are going or I'll be worrying all day long."

She leaned over and gave me a kiss. "Deal," she said. She walked out the door and into the first day of the rest of her life.

I have a picture of Zoë on the morning of her first day back at work. It's now all over the internet and easy to find. In it, she's sitting at our breakfast bar—the same one we sat at when we nearly broke up a few months before—and she's looking decidedly beautiful. She's wearing a lovely royal-blue sweater and a scarf from the scarf-sharing station I so carefully negotiated. She's smiling.

When I took the picture a few minutes before she left, I was smiling too. I smiled all the way to the door. I smiled when she leaned over and gave me a kiss. And the minute she closed the door and walked out to the car, I stopped smiling and almost started hyperventilating.

I kept my phone nearby and my car keys at the ready. I was convinced Zoë was going to run into some kind of trouble on her first day back and would need me to talk her down, either by phone or in person. Maybe people would avoid her because they wouldn't know what to say. Maybe someone who used to be friendly with her would treat her like a distant acquaintance.

I paced the floor endlessly.

Then I got a text.

"They decorated my cubicle!" Zoë wrote. "Look!" She sent me pictures.

When Zoë arrived at work, she'd nervously snaked her way through the cube farm and rounded the corner to her normally bland desk. But this time, it was filled with cheer. There were strings of colourful butterflies and shiny spiral decorations hanging from the shelves. There was a sprightly little plant next to her monitor. Her nameplate had been changed to the correct one and "Welcome back, Zoë!" was written in bold letters on her whiteboard. Her co-workers had even tidied up and organized her work area. New beginnings. A fresh start.

One person came by with a wrapped gift. Inside was a framed quote from Oscar Wilde that he had penned in calligraphy: "Be yourself: Everyone else is already taken."

"Well, fuck," I texted back to her. "Are you sobbing right now?"

"OMG, YES."

"Did you bring mascara?"

"Obviously. Who do you think you're talking to?"

She wrote me a few minutes later to tell me her eyes had been reapplied. "I've got to go," she said. "Emergency meeting upstairs. Guess it's back to business as usual!"

Zoë made her way upstairs to the conference room. A customer site had gone down, and as manager of the team responsible for some of the software being used, she needed to be briefed and start coming up with solutions. Her closest colleagues had made her feel welcome on her first day back, which she appreciated, but this meeting would be the true test of how the rest of the company—those in other departments—would treat her.

It certainly was. As it turned out, the meeting wasn't a meeting at all: it was a coming-out party. People from other departments had come to welcome her back.

Telecommunications companies have a reputation for being stuffy, conservative places with policies dating back to the Jurassic period. But not in this case. Zoë's company busted right out of that stereotype. While not every trans person will want a surprise party, her co-workers knew Zoë well enough to judge correctly.

What it boils down to—the parties, decorations, hugs and cupcakes—is inclusion. Zoë's colleagues wanted her to feel included, safe and reassured that she was still a valuable part of the team. That might look different or involve less fanfare in other work environments, but that's fine if it achieves the same result. There's a difference between showing a basic level of decency to another human being and going the extra mile. Following the human rights code and corporate policy on supporting LGBTQ people is basic decency. Letting your colleague know she's not only tolerated but fully accepted is going the extra mile.

That's what Zoë's colleagues did, and that's why, when she texted, "OMG, IT'S NOT A MEETING! IT'S A COMING OUT PARTY! *cry face*" I threw on my coat and ran out the door. I showed up at her work, hugged everyone I could find and took pictures of all the nice things they did for her that day. Then I put it all together in a blog post called "My Wife Came Out at Work and Her Co-Workers Threw Her a Party." I walked readers step by step through all the times Zoë had to reapply her mascara that day due to exceptional kindness.

I knew a handful of her work friends read my blog and I thought it would be nice to publicly thank them. I also hoped anyone else who read the post would get inspired to better support their trans co-workers. *Look what these people did and the difference it made! You can do it too! Here's a step-by-step guide to being awesome!* I expected it would be a cute little story read by a few hundred people. I must stress, once again, that I am a very poor estimator.

The post became one of the most widely read pieces I have ever written. It was featured on *BuzzFeed*, *Upworthy* and many other sites. One thing was becoming clear about sharing our family's journey through change: people love a happy story.

For the first few weeks after Zoë came out, we found ourselves in the media frenzy I had predicted. We weren't the first family to have more than one trans person in it, but we were one of the first to be public about it. People were also interested to hear that Zoë and I were staying together and were in a better place than before her transition began, which was not typical. We were pushing boundaries everywhere, and journalists wanted to talk to us about it.

We were careful about who we did interviews with. I did a search on every journalist who approached us, to see what that person's previous work was like. If it was ultra-conservative, transphobic or homophobic, we stayed away. If it was clear the journalist wanted to present our story in an honest and positive way, we were willing to talk. Our primary goal with all media was to show the world it was possible to thrive through transition and change. We wanted to normalize queer families.

We gave interviews to outlets such as Global News, *US Weekly*, *BuzzFeed*, *Redbook*, *Cosmo*, the *Independent*, the *Huffington Post* and various radio stations and podcasts. Each time, we made sure to set firm boundaries. No, we will not give you old pictures of what Zoë and Alexis used to look like. No, we will not give you old names. No, we will not talk about the state of anyone's genitals.

Setting boundaries is easy when you know what your goals are. When you're trying to get famous, you might have looser boundaries when talking to journalists. You might take more risks. But weren't trying to get famous. Our goal was to get a message out without harming the community we wanted to benefit. We wanted to highlight the positives in our story, while being candid about some of the struggles it took to get here. We didn't want to be gawked at or seen as some anomaly. We were just a family moving forward through change like many others. We didn't want media to show side-by-side comparisons of what Zoë and Alexis looked like then and now. The trans women in my family didn't believe that would send the right message; it would only perpetuate the idea they were a boy and a man who were becoming a girl and a woman.

They weren't. That's a big part of what we were trying to get across. Alexis and Zoë might have been labelled boys—they might have been born with the genitals associated with boys and men—but they never were. That's why they needed to transition.

My wife and daughter had chosen to move forward, beyond those old perceptions of them, and that is their right. If the media wanted to share our story, they would have to do it in a way that respected them. That was non-negotiable.

—

On April 8, just a few days after Zoë went back to work and life felt like it was finally starting to settle down again, my sister, Katie, texted me and said, "Your family is in the *Daily Mail*!"

She sent a link. I opened it. My body went cold.

The *Daily Mail* had emailed me twice in the past few days. They didn't ask for an interview but instead stated they were getting ready to publish a story about us and needed photos—including "before transition photos if available."

Nope. I wasn't giving them pictures. Not only for the reasons I've previously stated but also because the *Daily Mail* has a sordid history with the trans community and has published articles many deemed harmful.

I hoped that without photos, they wouldn't run the story. That was very naive of me.

As soon as the page loaded, my heart rose up into my throat. The header photo was a before-and-after shot of me and Zoë. The bigger photo was a recent one I had shared of the two of us. The one in the top corner was taken before transition. Other photos of my family were used too. They had deadnamed Zoë within the first few sentences. The entire article featured quotes from my blog and pieces of an interview I had granted to another publication. Furious, I yelled, "Assholes!" as I pounded my fists on the dining-room table and burst into tears.

Truth be told, I was more furious with myself. Where had they found those old pictures? Why hadn't I been more careful in making sure they were deleted? Where had they found Zoë's old name? How could we set such careful boundaries, only to have a publication walk all over them? I had royally screwed this up.

I called Zoë at work, crying so hard into the phone that for a minute I could barely breathe. She was upset at the news but not nearly as much as I was.

"It's okay," she said. "It's not your fault."

"It *is* my fault! It's my blog that caused all this."

"Your blog is doing a lot of good," Zoë said calmly. "Some people are just going to be awful, that's all."

"They used your old photos and your old name. Oh my God, Zoë. I can't believe they did that. I'm so sorry."

"I can believe it," she said. "Pre-transition photos get site hits. It's not the end of the world, though. It's not. It'll be fine."

Still completely guilt-ridden, I let her go and started doing damage control. First, I noticed that most of the photos the article had used were being shared directly from my Instagram account. I opened the app and deleted them. Next, I wrote a cease-and-desist letter to have the before-and-after photo removed from the site. Finally, I put statements out on Facebook and Twitter saying my family had not granted an interview to the *Daily Mail* and did not give them permission to use any of our photos. Then I cried some more. Once again, I thought about whether I would have shared so openly in 2014 if I knew that our family would be facing a second transition in the future. The answer was a loud and clear no.

A few years before, I had judged a family for pushing the boundaries of gender. Now it was my family being judged.

—

Don't read the comments. If there's a more solid piece of advice in the internet age, I don't know what it is.

You stop being people when you become a news story. You become a piece of information, something for others to consider and form opinions about, like a political candidate's platform or the designs at Fashion Week. Those reading the news sometimes forget that the people they're reading about are actual human beings.

I didn't want to look at the comments. I knew better. Readers can say some deplorable things about queer people in the news, and they go the extra mile when it's a trans person.

Zoë was, by all accounts, a success story. She'd transitioned as an educated, middle-class woman who kept her family and career. Not only that, her marriage was stronger and her connections to those around her were deeper. She was not harassed on the street or ignored by the neighbours. She lived a very typical, happy life. This ruffled some feathers so hard the bigotry fell right out of them. Internet trolls went out of their way to find something to be mean about.

I know a thing or two about trolls—the people who interject themselves into online conversations for the sole purpose of creating a stir or being cruel, often through insults and attacks. I know that social scientists have been studying them for the past few years and have concluded that most of them show worrisome traits. They seem to derive pleasure from knowing their words are hurting others. Trolls have always existed, but with the advent of the internet, they can get their jollies anonymously and in front of a larger audience.

But trolls are not always avoidable. Friends and family members would see our faces pop up on their Facebook feeds and excitedly tag us in the comments beneath the piece we were being featured in. *Hey, Amanda Jetté Knox! It's your beautiful fam!*

Each time, the jagged shores of the comments section would beckon me like a siren's call.

"Land, ho!" Emotional Amanda would call out.

"Nay, don't go forth!" Logical Amanda would yell. "You know what doom awaits us!"

"Balderdash!" Emotional Amanda would shout back, steering the ship toward the rocks. "What if it's filled with positivity and we miss out on that?"

"Fool," Logical Amanda would mumble under her breath. Then she would retreat to the lifeboat to await the inevitable shipwreck.

I shouldn't have read the comments.

"It looks like Gollum."

This was the first comment I read beneath the first article written about my wife's transition. The picture we had shared with the publication was a sepia-coloured selfie of Zoë and me, and it was one of the few at the time that didn't trigger massive dysphoria in her. She liked it. I liked it too. She looked lovely and at peace with herself, which was something I'd never seen captured in previous photos of her.

We're not stupid people; we knew sharing our story would leave her open to attacks. But we also knew the message we were trying to get out there was an important one, and this overruled most of the worry. When I saw that comment, though, worry came flooding back in. To see someone be so needlessly cruel to another human being wasn't new to me. Just another day on the internet, frankly. But this wasn't just another news story, and this wasn't being said about just anyone.

If Zoë saw this, what would it do to her?

I closed the tab and decided not to say anything. I make a lot of decisions like this. Trolls come crawling out from under their bridges to say revolting things about us, and I make a point of never speaking a word of it to anyone—especially my family members. More recently, a group of transphobes shared some of our family photos on a Facebook page so they could insult us— including our kids. Yes, adults made a point of attacking our children's looks and saying we had a "murky gene pool."

Everyone in my home knows the risks. We all know these things are said, but my family doesn't need to see every hurtful word. Once you see that stuff, you can't un-see it. One negative comment can linger in your brain for ages.

To make things worse, there's usually no way to win with trolls. If you defend yourself, they get off on it and keep pushing your buttons. If you report their account or delete their comment, they just create a new account, rally their little troll friends and replace that deleted comment with dozens of similar ones.

I've been told several times I need to grow a thicker skin. But that won't happen, and it's by conscious design. Sure, if I had a thicker skin, I could numb myself more easily to uncomfortable emotions. To turn off that caring, however, I would need to turn the pain inward. I did that for years, not wanting to deal with things that had happened to me as a child or avoiding a closer look at how unhappy I was in my marriage. I used food and other distractions to tamp down the pain. It only caused me more pain.

Author Brené Brown discusses this numbing behaviour in her books and videos. Her warning, which is based on both research and personal experience, is that trying to numb some feelings will numb them all. "We cannot selectively numb emotions," she writes in *The Gifts of Imperfection: Let Go of Who You Think You're Supposed to Be and Embrace Who You Are*. "When we numb the painful emotions, we also numb the positive ones."

We can't pick, in other words. We must turn it all off or leave it all on; there is no in-between. Our brains don't have an intricate way to filter feelings like that.

As much as I admire Brené and totally want to be best friends someday I didn't need to read her book to figure that out. I'd lived most of my life that way, which is why I refuse to do it any longer. I won't "armour up," as she puts it, to step into the arena. It will only hurt me in the long term. I won't become a shell of the person I really am. If I do that, I'm letting them win.

Instead of turning it off, I have two key reminders I use when I'm blindsided by hate. I try to teach them to my children.

First, other people's feelings, reactions and opinions are theirs to own and not mine. We each have a unique personality and experiences that have shaped our responses to what's happening around us. I have no control over how another person will react to a situation, and I can't be responsible for everyone's feelings about me and my family. I have no idea what other people are bringing to the table. Is it a nice ham? Internalized rage? Who knows? My job as a writer, speaker and advocate is to present my family's collective lived experience as a teachable moment. Whether other people choose to learn from that is up to them. Some will hang out in the back of the class and shoot spitballs no matter what I do. We're not all wired the same way, and recognizing this makes it easier to deal with the more disappointing responses.

Second, a lived experience is always more valid than an experience never lived. Many people like to share their opinions. That's fine. But I've learned that not all opinions are created equal. If people of colour share their experiences with racism, that will always be more valid than white people telling everyone what they think of racism and its effects. Why? Because we can't fully know what it's like to go through something unless we've gone through it ourselves.

The same is true when it comes to straight and cisgender people sharing opinions about queer people. When folks who have no lived experience make disparaging comments about my marriage to Zoë, her decision to transition and our support for our transgender teen, it makes it easier to disregard their opinions. I can have opinions about New Zealand, but I've never been there, you know?

Reminding myself of these things works most of the time, but not always. Occasionally, an anxiety attack, a short free fall into despair or a cry on someone's shoulder will follow. Once, after a targeted hate attack, I spent an evening crying and eating pizza in the basement while watching Meg Ryan movies. Another time, I adopted a rescue kitten. (Hey, you do what you need to do!) Eventually my brain remembers to do a validity check on those nasty, unfounded opinions and then it's over.

I also keep a running list of people I can rely on to catch me when I fall. These are the people I can say literally anything to in a difficult moment and know they'll stick around. The list is short, in part because trust takes a long time to build, and in part because not everyone is willing or equipped to sort through my years of emotional baggage. You need to have gone through a lot yourself to be able to handle this overflowing suitcase I'm lugging around.

The hate aimed at me and my family is ongoing. I constantly remind myself that people who say needlessly cruel things about other people reveal more about themselves than they do about their targets. Yes, the internet can be a brutal place, but it's also one of the best platforms we have to create change on a global scale. So I remain visibly online with my family's blessing, telling our story and hoping to help that change along for the next family in transition.

And while the internet can be vile, it can also be amusing. What I found most surprising about the conversations surrounding my relationship with Zoë is how focused others were on my sexuality. It was the topic du jour every time an article about us was shared. I watched as people posted questions, made assumptions and debated what this meant for me, the wife of a transitioning spouse. It was surreal to watch discussions about me happen without me.

What does this mean for the wife who isn't trans?

She can't be happy like that. She's straight.

How do you know she's straight?

Well, they've been married for almost twenty years. How could she not be?

She would have to be bisexual or pansexual. There's no other way this makes sense.

Maybe they're staying together for the kids.

Some marriages are platonic. I bet that's what this one will be like now. You know, separate bedrooms?

She's just trying to convince herself she's happy.

Is this the same Amanda Knox who was charged with murder in Italy?

That one still happens *all the time*. Two people can have the same name, internet. I couldn't help but laugh. What else can you do when the world is trying to figure you out?

I also regarded this as another teaching moment. I wasn't going to clarify my sexual orientation because it didn't matter. (Can't people just love other people? Do we have to put a label on everything and everyone? Love is love, folks. Simmer down.) But truth be told, a part of me had some figuring out to do in this department. Something deep inside had been stirring even before Zoë came out. Something that had been buried for most of my life.

I love the idea of bisexuality—or pansexuality, its more modern counterpart. Falling for hearts, not parts, is a lovely way to live. For a while, I identified with that concept. It seemed to fit. I was married to someone I thought was a man, and her transition to living as a woman did not spell the end of our romantic relationship. That screams bi or pan, right?

Except I wasn't sure that was true. Something about it didn't feel right, but the idea of exploring it made me deeply uncomfortable. I wasn't ready to take a closer look yet. So I kept the commenters—and myself—guessing. Maybe they would sort it out for me.

TWENTY-THREE

reality

COMING OUT CAN set you free. But freedom is an adjustment. Our entire family was discovering what this new normal looked like, and how the world saw us now.

A couple of days after Zoë returned to work, she had a meeting with a male co-worker to discuss some project deadlines. They both walked into a large boardroom and sat across from each other, he looking the same as the last time and Zoë looking entirely different. Before they got down to business, the co-worker spoke up.

"Can I be honest?" he asked.

"Of course," Zoë replied.

"This is weird for me."

"Okay," she said. "That's understandable."

"I don't have a problem with it or anything, I really don't," he assured her. "But if you feel like something's going on, or if I slip up and accidentally use the wrong name or pronouns, please know it's just me trying to adjust."

"It's fine," Zoë replied warmly. "Thank you for being so honest."

The co-worker visibly relaxed, and they went on with their meeting.

For the next few weeks and months, people at work would slip up, periodically using her old name in a meeting or calling her "he" or "him." She was patient, gently correcting them when she needed to and reminding them they need not frantically apologize for every misstep; she knew they were trying.

But not everyone tried. There were several men in another department who seemed to take issue with her transition but would never speak up about it for fear of being reprimanded. They were never exceptionally friendly prior to her coming out, but now they avoided her entirely. If they were chatting together and she walked by, they would go silent, casting disagreeable glances her way.

There were a couple of women, too, who regularly shot looks at Zoë. They seemed particularly uncomfortable when they saw her in the washroom. The feeling was mutual. The last thing she wanted was to be in a confined space with someone who didn't like her there.

Thankfully, most of the women in the company made her feel welcome. Whenever she entered the washroom, they would be sure to greet her with a smile and a quick chat, as they would with any other familiar female colleague. The few who appeared initially unhappy seemed to relax after witnessing a few of these interactions. Zoë was being accepted into the sisterhood, as it should be. Some were a little slower in that acceptance, but the keeners in the class were showing them how it's done.

Not long after returning to work, Zoë was at a male co-worker's desk, laughing and joking around as they often did a few times throughout the day. The man paused, mid-conversation, and said sadly, "You know, I'm really going to miss this."

"What do you mean?" Zoë asked.

"This," he said. "You and me. Our friendship."

"I'm not going anywhere," she replied. "We're still friends."

"Yeah," he said. "But it's going to be different now. We won't relate to each other in the same way."

"I'm still the same person," she assured him.

"I know. But our interactions will be different."

Zoë knew what he meant. He recognized that in our society, men and women interact often in different ways than people of the same gender do.

"I think you'll find our friendship is a whole lot better now that I'm not hiding a part of who I am anymore," Zoë stated confidently.

In the end, she was right. Their relationship wasn't negatively impacted by her transition. It became more real. They've only grown closer since.

—

Hollywood was also feeling a lot closer than it used to be. We received a request from a casting agent in Los Angeles who wanted us to audition for a new reality show on a major US network.

The premise of the show sounded promising: it would tell the stories of a handful of families, each going through different changes, such as transition or adoption. But we were hesitant. Reality shows tend to be anything but realistic; the quest for ratings often dictates what stories are told. More drama equals more viewership. We were up front about how mundane our family life is. "Things have settled down a lot," I explained to the casting agent. "We're very boring. At this point, we're a typical family that just happens to have two trans people in it."

"That's exactly what our client is hoping for," she told us. "The producers want to see the typicality because it will normalize trans experiences. You can show America how happy you can be through these changes."

Well, that sounded lovely. But we still weren't sold.

Zoë and I figured we had nothing to lose by auditioning via Skype, however. We weren't committing to anything, and going through the process would be a fun experience. We hopped on the call and spent about an hour with the agent and one of her colleagues. Our conversation was recorded and turned into a video for the show's producers.

Surprisingly, we were a hit with both the producers and the network executives. "This is the first time this network has been willing to work with a Canadian family," the agent told us. "The fact they're willing to send a camera crew to Ottawa to film a season is significant. You really impressed them!"

Television is a fickle and highly competitive industry. We knew we were one of several families being considered for this opportunity, and we were shocked we had made the cut. But otherwise, we still weren't sure how we felt about it.

"The producers will be in touch with a contract for you to look over," the casting agent explained. "Congratulations!"

"This could be good, right?" I said to Zoë. "Maybe?"

"It could," she replied. "Let's see what the contract looks like."

When it finally arrived, it was anything but good.

"Have you read this yet?" my wife asked me. "This contract is terrifying."

We were sitting on the back deck, a warm summer breeze cutting the evening humidity. I had sent the papers to her to look over, as she was better with fine print. I'm glad I did. Her laptop sat on the table, illuminating the concern on her face.

"They want to install cameras all over the house," she said. "Including the bathroom."

"What? Like *Big Brother*?" I was stunned. "We have kids. They know this, right?"

"And there's no way to turn them off," she continued. "They control that function, not us."

It got even more invasive. They could use the footage in any way they wished, including creating personas for us through editing that could paint us in a bad light. They could dictate what media outlets we spoke to, and what we spoke to them about. And for all of this, we would get paid a one-time "location fee" of US$10,000 for the entire season. This was not a salary, the contract specified, as our family would be doing this for exposure. Technically, we wouldn't even be getting paid.

I couldn't believe people actually signed contracts like this. "This is a joke, right?"

We wrote the company to turn down the "opportunity," then had a good laugh at the absurdity of it all over a glass of wine. The production company tried to assure us this was a standard reality contract, and we could negotiate it to better suit our needs, including around compensation and where the cameras would be placed. But it was clear to us that taking part in this project would not suit our family's needs at all—nor would it serve to normalize transgender issues.

We would later decline two other reality-show ideas for the same reason. We're not here for society to gawk at. We want to educate through visibility, not be exploited or manipulated for ratings. Reaching new demographics through media is impor-tant, and television can get it right. But often it still gets it wrong.

A while back, a friend who works in media gave me an impor-tant piece of advice: "Remember this is *your* story, and you get to control how much of it you tell and how you tell it." We're happy to be visible, but on our own terms.

"sir"

BECAUSE ALEXIS WAS young when she started her transition, and therefore was given hormone blockers before her natal puberty caused too many typically masculine changes, she is always seen by the people she interacts with as a girl. This is the gift of being able to come out at a young age, and to receive good family and medical support when you do.

Not everyone is so fortunate, particularly when transitioning as an adult. For a while after Zoë socially transitioned, but before hormone therapy reshaped her face and gave it a more feminine look, she was regularly misgendered by others. It cut through her each time.

There were the usual slip-ups from people she had known pre-transition: a few family members, friends and co-workers fumbled over names and pronouns as their brains rewired themselves. While this could sting a little, what hurt most were the assumptions of people who didn't know her and didn't immediately recognize her as a woman. Those encounters were painful reminders of a former life.

Zoë had spent months working on her voice: she was trying to raise the pitch and change the resonance and intonation. She had been working with a speech therapist and was quite proud of how far she had come. She was feeling particularly confident one day when I asked if we could swing by the drive-through for coffee. It was one of the lovely lighter days, when dysphoria hadn't taken hold of her and we were enjoying life together. The sun was shining, we had a playlist going, and all we needed was some caffeine to make it perfect.

"Welcome to *Coffee-place-I'm-not-naming-here.* Can I take your order?" the outdoor speaker asked.

"Hi," said Zoë cheerily. "Can I get a medium with one cream and a small black decaf?"

"Sure," said the chipper voice behind the speaker. "Drive up to the window and someone will see you there. Have a nice day, sir."

Sir. Three letters that sucker-punched our near-perfect day in the stomach.

Zoë looked at me, stricken. "Sir. He called me sir."

"Honey . . ." I started, searching for the right words to make this better.

"Does my voice sound *that* masculine?"

"No!" I replied, hoping she could hear the sincerity in my words. With diligent daily practice, her voice had climbed to the lower range of the average cisgender woman. "I don't know why he said that. Honest."

But my reassurances weren't powerful enough to undo the damage that had been done by this stranger's one word. My wife looked shattered by the time we got to the drive-through window. She didn't make eye contact with the cashier. "Thank you," she practically whispered before driving away. She was holding back tears.

Zoë wanted not only to live as the woman she's always been but also to be seen as one by the rest of society. To be seen as a woman would mean being accepted and safe. It would mean never having to justify or validate her gender to anyone, or be viewed as "other." My womanhood had never been called into question, and until I'd supported two people through transition, I had never considered how damaging that invalidation could be.

I was watching that damage unfold right now. She was gutted, her feelings spilling out in front of me. The confidence she had built up over the past few weeks was crumbling. Our perfect day ended up with her sitting in the bedroom, hiding from the world. I sat beside her and struggled to find the words—any words—to make things better. The hole she had crawled into was so deep I wasn't able to reach down far enough to pull her out. I could only wait at the top and shine a light down.

I can't take the pain away when someone misgenders Zoë. All I can do is be there for her in the short term while working in the longer term to help my fellow cis people gain a broader understanding of gender. Most of the time, we misgender trans and non-binary people without malice. We're either learning new pronouns for someone or making assumptions about gender based on what we've been taught. Most of us have been taught to assume someone is either a man or a woman. We do this by picking up on physical characteristics, dress, voice and even subtle mannerisms. We've done this for years in Western society, not realizing we were sometimes getting it wrong and causing real harm.

To complicate matters, we not only make these gender assumptions but also declare them as an act of respect. Calling someone "sir," "miss" or the dreaded "ma'am" (which I'm greeted with far more these days) is strongly encouraged, if not outright enforced, in many customer-service jobs. But because gender isn't as clear-cut as society once thought, it's time to start rethinking our ideas of politeness.

There are many genderless ways to greet people without being rude. Here are a few samples:

"Hello, how are you today?"

"Hi! Can I help you find anything?"

"Hello, folks. How's everyone doing today?"

"Are the two of you ready to order?"

Yes, Alexis was once thrilled to bits at a coffee shop drive-through window when the server got her gender right. But Zoë's confidence took a hit when someone got hers wrong in the same circumstance. We don't need to guess at someone's gender to be kind. In fact, it might be kinder and simpler if we don't.

The world is changing. More people are coming out than ever, and our society needs to evolve along with them. Rather than insisting that trans and non-binary people meet cisgender criteria, let's change our ideas of gender and be more inclusive. That would allow everyone—trans and cis people alike—to live with fewer restraints. Change, I'm discovering, is refreshing.

For now, though, Zoë and I take turns being there for each other during our respective tumbles into the darkness. I'll wait at the top all day if I need to, holding the light and extending a hand down for when she eventually grabs it. She does the same for me. I love her through it. She loves me through it. Our relationship is built on shared experiences, and not all of them are good. But each one of these painful moments makes us stronger. There's a trust in falling apart in front of someone and allowing her the honour of being there for you. For years, Zoë didn't put that trust in me. Everything inside screamed to hold back or risk losing me. I don't blame her; she was almost right about that. But I'm glad she trusts me today. I'll hold her while she cries any day she needs me to.

But she doesn't need me to very often these days. I would much rather hold her while she smiles. She has a beautiful smile.

TWENTY-FIVE

whole

OUR SOCIETY IS obsessed with trans people's genitals.

What is or isn't between a person's legs seems to govern how much we accept them, judge them or fear them. We try to pass laws restricting where trans people can go to the bathroom, where they can change clothes, what shelters they can stay in and even what prisons should house them.

A journalist once asked my twelve-year-old about her future plans for surgery. When I stepped in to stop it, the journalist turned to me and said, "Can I ask *you* about her plans, then?"

No, you cannot. Fixating on a child's genitals is never appropriate, whether that child is trans or not. That should be common sense. Sadly, it isn't. It's weird, and frankly a little creepy, how much people care.

This is why, for the entirety of my family's time sharing our story publicly, none of us has ever discussed whether Alexis or Zoë has had or will have gender-affirming surgery. People have made countless assumptions about what's between my wife's legs, often as an attempt to invalidate her womanhood or my attraction to her. We've refused to comment on or clarify those assumptions. It is no one else's business.

Some people can't wait for surgery; they want it yesterday. Some desperately want it but can't get it for medical or financial reasons. Some have no interest whatsoever; they feel completely comfortable with the parts they were born with. Choosing to forgo gender-affirming surgery—there are several kinds, but we tend to fixate on the lower half, or "bottom surgery"—does not negate that person's gender identity. Some women have penises and some men have vulvas. I've met plenty, and I know they have these parts only because they've chosen to disclose that information. It does not take away from who they are.

That being said, there is one good reason to discuss surgical procedures: for some, they are absolutely necessary and life-saving. If these procedures are never discussed—if no one shares their importance—it makes it easier for governments and insurance companies to deem them cosmetic and unnecessary. Some of them already are. As I've said before, trans people who need surgery but face long wait times or are unable to get it at all have an increased risk of suicide. We need to keep these surgeries funded and make them more accessible.

For this reason alone, this chapter exists.

—

Zoë, the once-hidden girl from Peterborough, was finally living in the open. Blockers had stopped her testosterone production, and estrogen was doing the right things to her body—albeit much later than she would have liked. After more than four decades of shame and secrecy, everything was moving in the right direction. Not only that, but her family still loved her, her co-workers had accepted her and the neighbours still chatted with her without skipping a beat. By all accounts, her transition had been fairly smooth.

She had difficult days, certainly. Dysphoria would take over at the most expected and unexpected times. Being misgendered on the phone would do it—that was expected. But she also might go to bed one night, happy with what was reflected in the mirror, only to wake up hating what she saw the next morning. Staring back at her wouldn't be the beautiful woman she saw hours before, but the person she used to be—the one who didn't fit and brought her pain. Those days were hard. She would fight her way through them the best she could. But the fight was harder because there was still a part of her that triggered those feelings so easily.

After assessments, hormones, social transition and name and gender marker changes, there was just one more thing to do, one thing to put right. It would take many steps to get there. She needed a whole new psychological and medical assessment. She required letters from her psychologist, endocrinologist and family doctor. She needed to send blood-work results, photos and a pile of papers to a small Montreal surgical clinic that specialized in exactly what she was looking for. She had less of a wait than some people she had talked to, but still far too long.

One evening, while we were drinking wine with two friends, an email popped up on Zoë's phone. And just like the message from Alexis three years earlier, this one was life-changing. Her surgery date was May 23, 2017, just a few weeks away. She could barely contain her joy, and neither could those of us around her.

On May 21, we arrived at a three-storey bed and breakfast in Montreal, excited and nervous. We spent time meeting other trans women who had come for the same reason, and bonds were quickly formed. They were sharing a deeply personal and unique experience. The entire stay was a well-oiled machine—the clinic even sent a taxi to pick us up the morning of her surgery and take us to the hospital.

"This is it," Zoë said as she tucked her hair into the surgical cap. She smiled one last time and left the room, walking up a flight of stairs to greet the specialists who would finally help her feel complete.

I drove to a nearby Tim Hortons to grab a quick lunch before returning to the hospital. I didn't want to miss Zoë getting out of surgery. I paced the main floor, watching trans people climb gingerly out of bed and shuffle the halls with the help of nursing staff. I saw on their faces the pain of moving about after a major surgery, but mixed in with the discomfort was an unmistakable look of peace. I was so moved I had to look away. The last thing I wanted to do was stare, but it was a beautiful sight. I only hoped Zoë would feel this way too.

Like many cisgender people, I used to question why anyone would want to have such a delicate area completely reworked. But after living through the transition with Zoë and watching her struggle, I got it. This was a critical step in her journey. It wasn't a desire—it was a need that could vastly improve her life.

After what seemed like far too long (it was only about four hours), a nurse came to tell me that Zoë was in recovery, slowly waking up. I breathed a huge sigh of relief.

An hour or so later, my wife was wheeled into the room. Drugged and dazed, she smiled from her bed.

"Honey, it's done," she said. "Can you believe it? I'm so happy."

"Oh, babe. I'm so happy for you too," I replied. Because there, amid the high from the drugs, was that unmistakable look of peace. She could fully live her life now.

There's a lot of crying in our story. That day was no exception. But it was the happy kind of crying.

TWENTY-SIX

resolve

"WE SHOULD GET MARRIED AGAIN," I had said to Zoë on one of our nature walks a few months before her surgery. Fall was coming to Ottawa and we were trying to make the most of the warm weather before the snow and frigid temperatures arrived.

"Like a vow renewal?" she asked.

"Yeah. For our twentieth anniversary."

"Okay," she said, mulling the idea over. "What would that look like?"

"Whatever we want it to look like," I replied. "That seems to be the running theme of our relationship anyway."

She tried to elbow me playfully. I dodged it, giggling. I was still going to the gym, was still eating healthy portions and had been maintaining a fifty-pound weight loss with ease. Strength training and walking were a big part of my life. I wasn't exactly a small person, but I was a hell of a lot faster. She would have to try harder.

"Hey, I'd get to wear a dress," she said.

"Yes, you would!"

When we got married in 1997, she had stuffed herself into a rented tuxedo and spent the next eighteen years trying to be my husband. It ended up being a painful experience for both of us. That pain came out in some obvious ways, and some less obvious ones. Case in point: never once in those eighteen years did we display a wedding photo. They had always been tucked away in a box and a half-finished wedding album. We took them out from time to time to show the kids, but they were otherwise neglected.

We also never wore our wedding rings. Because we were living below the poverty line at the time, we had bought them, mismatched, from a pawnshop. Those were sitting in a box too. I know how special wedding rings are for some people; they're worn with a sense of pride. We never had that.

It's easy to blame an unhappy marriage on the obvious. In this case, Zoë's need to transition was the glaring culprit. I can pinpoint many times when her sullen moods and angry outbursts took a toll on our relationship. But there's more to this story. There's a less obvious but just as damaging culprit. Alexis and Zoë weren't the only ones in dark closets for too long.

Here's the reality I denied myself for forty years: I'm gay. A big ol' lesbian. Dykeville, USA (well, Canada).

I should have figured this out ages ago. The biggest indicator was that I was instantly and solely attracted to girls and women from a young age. The edgy punk chicks at my school. Daisy Duke and her short shorts from *The Dukes of Hazard*. Wonder Woman and that whip of hers. Basically the entire cast of *Charlie's Angels*. Sure, I could recognize a good-looking guy, but he didn't do it for me in the same way.

Maybe I would have admitted this sooner if I hadn't thrown

myself into the closet and slammed it shut with a dozen locks after one terrible incident. In my early teen years, I fooled around with a female friend and we got caught in the act. Her mom pulled us into the kitchen, sat us down and laid a heap of guilt on us.

"What you did was wrong," she said, incensed. "It's disgusting and I'm disappointed. You're both good girls raised in good homes. Why would you do something like that? Do you want to go to hell?"

I glanced over at the cross hanging above the door frame. Years of Catholic school teachings and the odd Sunday school lesson had taught me this too. Man does not lie with man. Woman does not lie with woman. This is not how it's done. Except it sure felt damn good to do it.

I could hear my friend sniffling quietly as her mom chastised us. We couldn't look at each other.

"I understand being curious at your age. But I never want you to do that again," she said to her daughter with absolute assertion. Then she turned to me. "Amanda, look at me."

I looked up hesitantly and met her eyes.

"I don't want to get you in trouble over one mistake. If you promise me this won't happen again, I won't tell your parents."

"I promise," I said right away. "I'm sorry. It definitely won't happen again." I meant every word.

"Good," her mother replied. "Then we'll keep this to ourselves."

That was the last time I ever set foot in that kitchen or spent time with that friend. I left quickly, feeling like I had dodged a sizable bullet. I couldn't imagine my mom getting a phone call like that, or the conversation that would have ensued. My mind played through various scenarios. None of them were good.

My friend went on to marry a man and have children. I went on to marry someone I thought was a man and have children too. My guess is our little tryst was nothing more than some experimenting for her—lots of teens do that. But it was more than that for me. I was attracted to her, and everything about our time together felt right. Everything about my time with guys afterward felt wrong. But it was easy to ignore those urges and convince myself I was straight—at least for a while. Society is built on straightness. Every movie, every TV show and our terribly limited sex-ed curriculum in the late eighties and early nineties taught me I was supposed to fall for guys, marry one of them and have his babies. It was expected of me. To do anything else would make me stand out. That was the last thing I wanted.

I dated guys who showed interest in me, however unhealthily, and the intoxicating attention they gave me filled the void where attraction should be. I was intimate with some of them to keep them from leaving me because being left was a blow to my already cracked foundation. I married Zoë because that was the closest to a serious attraction I had experienced with someone I thought was a guy. I thought that was what being in love felt like.

Over time, I realized I wasn't happy, but it was easy for me to blame her unhappiness for my own. She was miserable trying to live that life, and I fell into the role of victim. Poor Amanda, raising three kids with someone who wasn't buying in. Poor Amanda, who would be so much happier if she was with a guy who wanted what they had.

Poor Amanda, who developed crushes exclusively on women, fantasized about them and admitted to a friend when things were rocky that should she ever find herself single again, she would only date women. After the look my friend gave me, I remember wishing I could take the words back. I had revealed too much.

After Zoë came out, I didn't think our relationship would survive. But it wasn't because she was a woman. It was because of the long history of struggle between us and my worry, deep down, that I might not be attracted to her. Attraction between two people is an imperfect science, after all. When she lived as a man, I could appreciate that she was good-looking. But what would she look like with more feminine features?

As it turns out, massively hot. She simply glows. The further down the path of transition she went, the more my attraction grew. Not only is she more physically beautiful, with a body I appreciate on a level I never could in a more masculine form, but she smiles more, laughs more and is very funny. I love everything about her, from the gentle way she holds me to the softness of her skin. I love my wife.

I am *in love* with my wife in every way. I can't take my eyes off her when she walks down the stairs looking ready for a night out. My heart skips a beat when she kisses me. I can't wait to see her at the end of a long day, to spend time with her and make her laugh. That is what I had missed out on in our previous incarnation.

When people started speculating about my sexuality online after our story broke, I kept quiet about where I stood, not only to make a point about respecting people's sexual orientations but also to protect myself from shame. I couldn't admit I was a lesbian—the mere thought sent me back to that kitchen, and I could almost feel the disapproving look from my friend's mother. Instead, I hid that reality and played a role to make society happy.

The truth is, if Zoë hadn't come out, our marriage would have either hobbled along for a lifetime with neither of us feeling good in it or ended when I admitted to myself I was gay. I was getting close to doing that—she just pushed me out of the closet a little sooner than expected.

Because Zoë's living her truth, I'm finally able to live mine. This is the life I should have had all along. I'm a lesbian. Being able to say it, to own it and to be proud of it only makes my foundation stronger.

I wish the rest of the world understood this. It would make our lives a little easier. In fact, other than when I'm called a child abuser for affirming my trans teen, one of the things I get attacked for the most is saying I'm a lesbian. Anti-trans activists regularly criticize me online for this declaration. Why? Because they don't accept trans women as women, and therefore they believe I'm straight and resent me saying otherwise.

Obviously, this just makes me plant my lesbian flag on every hill I can find. If there's one thing I can't stand, it's bigotry in all its forms.

People don't get to decide what my sexual orientation is, and they also don't get to exclude trans women from womanhood. This type of trans-exclusionary behaviour is extremely damaging to an already marginalized community. Telling me I'm not a lesbian is another way to invalidate my wife's gender. To get their point across, they misgender Zoë and call her my husband, a "confused man who gets turned on by pretending to be a woman." They fetishize her, ridicule her.

They say I'm along for the ride, indulging her fantasy to keep our marriage afloat. They call me names, tell me I'm lying to myself and everyone else. They say I'm pretending to be gay and "erasing real lesbians." They even make up things I've supposedly said to try to discredit me to my growing audience of readers and online followers. The more visible we get, the more they try to take us down.

This small but vocal and organized group of anti-trans activists—many of whom proudly call themselves "gender-critical"—focus intensely on denying the validity of transgender experiences. While many are straight, some are part of the lesbian, gay and bisexual communities—heartbreaking proof that not all of us are in this together. These people often claim that trans men are simply confused lesbians, and that trans women are perverts playing dress-up. They claim an invasion of women's spaces, and the indoctrination of children into the "trans ideology." It's confusing and ugly rhetoric, based largely on unfounded fears and misconceptions.

Our love threatens them. Our story frightens them. It undoes the work they try to do. They want to make trans people out to be unlovable monsters, not wonderful partners, caring parents and happy human beings.

On one occasion, after I had talked about the vileness of their attacks and even the threats I had received, one tweeted me and said if I would just admit I'm not a lesbian, they would leave me alone.

In other words, if I just backed down, they would stop bullying me.

She clearly doesn't know me.

Unfortunately for her and the others of that ilk, I spent my formative years dealing with bullies. I know them well. I've been attacked from every angle and I know all the tricks. I nearly ended my life because of them, then I spent years cultivating the resiliency I needed to push beyond that pain.

My friend, I was literally set on fucking fire. Do you honestly think calling me a few bad words is going to make me stop speaking out for LGBTQ rights? *Please.*

I'm here for the long haul. This is the fight life set me up to do. I don't know if I believe in a higher power, but I know the universe took a bullied girl who was afraid of change and nonconformity, threw her into one of the most misunderstood family situations on the planet and made her face her fears. How could I not learn to be a better person? How could I not get stronger? I have an abundance of strength in my own home to draw from every day.

I was built for this. I'm not going anywhere.

One day, Jackson, Zoë and I were all sitting on the couch in the living room when our phones lit up in succession. They were Facebook messages from the same unknown individual. I read mine first. It was a string of insults and slurs about how sick my family was, how disgusting my wife and child were, and how we were damaging our other children. Zoë had received something similar.

"Jackson, please hand me your phone," I asked calmly.

"Why?" he asked, picking it up from the coffee table in front of him.

"Someone has sent you a terrible message and I'm going to delete it."

"One of your 'admirers,' Mom?" he inquired sarcastically. He handed it over.

"I'm really sorry, buddy. I'm disgusted someone would send

this to you," I said, reading it to myself. It was all about how dysfunctional our family was, and how Jackson was going to be messed up for the rest of his life. I nuked it and blocked the person.

"Whatever," he said. "Get a hobby, guy. I'm not the one who's trolling kids." He gave us both a hug and we went back to watching TV.

Our children are just fine, thanks.

I have had to file police reports on two separate occasions after receiving threats. Those are just the ones I've bothered to report. One was sent to my daughter's middle school after the release of the Microsoft video. Another was sent directly to me on Facebook messenger. It told me I had a giant target on my back.

Going on high alert is stressful. The kids couldn't go anywhere alone for a while. I had to talk to teachers and principals about taking increased security measures. I made sure all our doors and windows were locked. I was jumpy in public and didn't even enjoy my usual trips to the grocery store.

After the second time, I began taking antidepressants again and have stayed on them since. Life is more manageable this way. But we can't—and don't—live our lives in fear. We're careful about sharing too much personal information online, but we don't hide from our community. Zoë and I often walk hand in hand when we take the dogs out, and just about everyone, young and old, greets us with a smile. Our kids rule the neighbourhood on bikes, scooters and skateboards. A pride flag waves proudly in our front garden.

Fear does not win in this house, on this street or in this city. Love does.

TWENTY-SEVEN

ripples

"MY DRESS IS HERE!" Zoë shouted excitedly from the front door.

It was a few weeks before our vow renewal. We had both taken a big gamble and ordered our dresses online. She brought the box containing hers up to the bedroom and opened it. I took my dress, which had arrived a few days before, out of the closet and put it up next to hers.

The gamble had not paid off.

"These don't go together," I said, panic mounting in my voice.

"Sure, they do," she said. "If you maybe . . . um, if we . . ." She trailed off, moving her dress to one side of mine then the other as I shook my head.

"The fabrics and styles are completely different," I said. "And yours doesn't look like the pictures."

As cute as it was, Zoë's dress was not cute in the way the website photos had said it would be. It was shorter and whiter than we had been led to believe. Next to mine—a lacy, creamy, garden party dress with dainty pink flowers—it looked completely out of place.

"You're right," she said. "This is a fashion disaster."

Weddings between two feminine-presenting—or femme—lesbians, I decided, were complicated. If one of us had wanted to wear a suit, this would be much easier. But because neither of us did, we had to find two dresses that not only complemented our different body types but also looked great together. No small feat.

"What should we do?" Zoë asked. "Return them?"

"I can't return my dress!" I exclaimed. "Do you know how hard it is to find one you feel great in when you're a full-figured woman who's had three kids?"

"I like my dress too," she said, staring at it longingly. "I don't want to send it back."

"I know, but you look good in *everything*," I said, a little too resentfully. "You have the body of a model."

"Not true!"

"Please." I rolled my eyes. "Going dress shopping with you is hard only because they all look so nice on you that you can't decide which one to buy. What a problem to have."

"That's such an exaggeration!" she fired back.

Things were getting heated. There was only one thing to do.

"That's it," I said, putting my hand up to stop the conversation. "We need to settle this with a dress-off."

"A what?"

"A dress-off," I declared. "We both try on our dresses, and whoever wears hers best gets to keep it."

"Deal," she replied competitively, and started throwing off her clothes.

Within a couple of minutes, we were zipping up our wedding wear in front of the mirror.

"Wow," said Zoë, looking at me. "You really do look beautiful in that dress. It's perfect on you."

"Thanks," I replied, blushing. "And you . . . uh . . ." I stopped. There was no use in lying.

"I look terrible in this dress," she said.

"I didn't want to say it." I winced. Zoë, who rocked every dress I had ever seen her in, looked like a cotton ball with legs. The dress was too short. It didn't hang well on her at all, and it was decidedly not meant for taller women, no matter what the website promised.

"You win," she sighed. "I'll box this up. Let's hit the mall tomorrow."

Given how stunning my wife is, this is likely the only dress-off I will ever win. But I will hold it over her head for a very long time.

—

I have by my desk a wall filled with sticky notes. Each one has a message I've transcribed from an email, tweet, text, Facebook message or in-person conversation where someone has told me that the advocacy work I do and our family's story has made a difference. There are dozens of them, and all of them are along these lines:

"You're a strong role model for parents, resilient children and youth."

"Thank you for being the voice for so many of us."

"You're one of the reasons I didn't kill myself."

"Your family is saving lives with what you're doing. Not all heroes wear capes."

If you had asked me years ago what I would be doing with my life, I never could have guessed this. The ideas I had for careers ranged from veterinarian to computer hardware engineer to journalist. None of my dreams involved LGBTQ advocacy.

I did not expect to speak in front of thousands of people at WE Day Vancouver with my amazing trans kid. In November 2016, we took the stage at this celebration of young changemakers with Microsoft's vice-president of worldwide education to discuss our online advocacy work. When I asked the audience if acceptance and understanding for trans people was finally happening, eighteen thousand people cheered. Loudly. It was beautiful.

I could never have guessed I would be the keynote speaker in Banff on International Women's Day, discussing the importance of lifting up all women, including our transgender sisters.

I never thought our whole family would be invited to meet Prime Minister Justin Trudeau on the day the federal government's trans rights bill was tabled. His commitment to LGBTQ rights could be felt in every word he spoke to us. He thanked us for our visibility, and we thanked him for keeping his campaign promise to make the country safer for trans people.

I couldn't have predicted the embarrassing moment when I cried with joy in Justice Minister Jody Wilson-Raybould's arms when the trans rights bill was passed into law in June 2017. After years of stalled and failed bills and after months of debate in Parliament and in the media, I was overwhelmed by the relief of knowing my daughter would grow up with laws protecting her.

I never expected to speak in the Reading Room on Parliament Hill for the House of Commons' first Pride Month celebrations. It was an honour to be asked, and the fact I was speaks volumes about the work done by those who came before us, the ones who did the hard labour to get society to a place where Pride is recognized and a gay woman with a trans wife and daughter would even be considered someone worth listening to.

Once I was a little girl who was sunny, funny and charming. My name meant "worthy of love," but the world made me feel anything but. The light nearly went out of my life from hopelessness. I came back from that, but I spent years keeping that light dim, just wanting to fit in and be accepted. I wanted to be worthy of love, and I thought being like everyone else was the key.

Thankfully, life didn't let me keep believing that.

As it turns out, loving my family fiercely and unconditionally is what gives me the love I was craving. Fighting for the rights of families like mine is one of the ways I've learned to love myself. It's helped me let go of my past and heal by using what I've learned through trial and trauma. I no longer live like the girl set on fire. I no longer live like the girl who lost her virginity to rape. I no longer live in shame because I was a young mom and never realized the dreams I had for myself. I'm not the woman-who-rips-up-her-lawn-to-make-the-neighbours-happy anymore.

My life reflects exactly who I am: unconventional. And now I get to use what I've learned to help other people who are unconventional in their own ways. It's the very best sort of life.

I might do the bulk of the public advocacy work in my family, but that doesn't mean the rest of the Knox crew isn't actively changing the world too. Alexis and Zoë are happy to live their lives quietly, going to school and work, spending time with friends and family, doing a bit of advocacy here and there but otherwise just *living*. They don't try to hide who they are, but they don't make a big deal out of it either. The way they change the world is through example. They continue to call into question old stereotypes about trans people and defy statistics. They're happy, loved and successful in what they do. They enjoy relative stability and an abundance of support from their community. We need positive examples like them in the world, which is why they're willing to let the writer and storyteller in the family share parts of their lives with others.

Aerik and Jackson are two of the most loving young men I've ever met. They chose to lead with love when their sister and mama came out, rather than with anger or resentment. It hasn't always been easy.

One day, Aerik told his mama he was struggling with her transition. "I thought I had a father, and then I didn't. I looked up to you as my male role model. What does that mean for me now?"

Zoë nodded empathetically. She thought for a moment and said, "You know, everything you learned from me about becoming a good man is still valid. All that compassion, sensitivity and strength is still there. Some guys don't learn that from other guys—they learn it from the strong women in their lives."

A perfectly stated and abundantly satisfactory answer. Guys with two moms can be amazing too.

Jackson, whose young life changed so much, has made sure to always put love first, even while processing and accepting that change. He was the first to switch pronouns with no mistakes and the first to start cracking "two moms" jokes. He insists that those around him be open-minded and accepting of LGBTQ people, and he is quick to educate them when they are not. He's my little hero.

Soon after Zoë came out, I asked Jackson and Alexis how things were going at school. Were people accepting of the news they had two moms?

"Oh yeah," Alexis said. "Having gay parents is cool now."

"It's true!" Jackson agreed. "People keep saying to me, 'Aww! I wish I had two moms!'"

"Is everyone like that?" I asked.

"Well," Jackson replied, "there is this one kid who says you can't have two moms or two dads. Everyone has to have a mom and a dad or they don't exist."

"That must be frustrating," I empathized.

"Only for him." He grinned. "Every time I talk about my family in class now, I make a point of saying 'my moms,' whenever I can. I figure it'll eventually sink in."

I gave him a high-five.

My family members are the ones creating change. I'm just the storyteller.

Our story has reached around the world. I regularly get emails from people in countries where trans rights are non-existent or under attack. Some feel scared and hopeless. Some find hope in stories like ours. Some ask me for advice, although I don't always know what to say. Sometimes all I can do is listen. Sometimes that's enough.

I once heard from a trans woman in Finland who had used our story as a springboard to come out to her wife. We ended up hosting them in our home for a few months, along with their baby. They came to Canada to escape the rampant transphobia in their otherwise progressive country. We gave them a place to stay and food to eat, helped raise funds for legal proceedings, and connected them to LGBTQ resources and community. Ultimately, they lost their asylum claim and had to return home. It broke our hearts. Last I heard, things were difficult for them.

We've connected with plenty of local people too. I've taken several parents of newly out trans kids to an in-person support group so they could see that they're in good company. Zoë and I have met several strangers who are trying to come to terms with a loved one's transition—or their own. Sometimes, you just need to know you're not alone, and sitting with another person who's been there is the first step in acceptance.

One Ottawa trans woman reached out to me after reading Zoë's work story. It made her realize she could no longer keep lying to herself. She needed to have the freedom the woman in the story had. We met for lunch when she was at the beginning of her journey, still using a male name and male pronouns, still relatively quiet and introverted. Today, she's an energetic, extroverted person, living as the woman she always knew she was. Bonus: we're great friends.

A woman who had been reading my blog for years and would share parts of it with her spouse got in touch with me when that spouse came out to her as a trans woman. "I never thought what I was reading in your blog would become my own life," she said to me. We invited them over to meet us and other families in similar situations. They ended up moving down the street, and I often bring my dog over to play with theirs.

We get stopped by people who recognize us on the street, in the store, at our kids' schools, at the gym, in restaurants and doctors' offices. Nearly every interaction is positive, and sometimes involves hugs.

"Thank you for teaching me about families like yours."

"My nephew came out last week and I was able to send his mom your blog."

"I don't have any trans people that I know of in my life, but learning about your family helped me understand why I need to care about their rights and safety anyway."

Once again, this is the power of visibility. This is what fuels the work we do and helps us push through the negativity. I know we're making a difference. It's not always fun and it's not always comfortable, but when we look at the big picture, it's always rewarding.

Whenever I'm having a bad day, I read the wall of sticky notes. I run my fingers along the words, written in my best (and yet still terrible) handwriting, and I smile. Even on the worst days, I smile. Each one is meaningful.

Yes, there have been some big opportunities and cool experiences in the past few years. But they pale in comparison to what's important: our family's happiness, the friendships we've made, the impact we're having, the community we're growing. These are the reasons we continue living as openly as we do.

TWENTY-EIGHT

renewal

"ARE YOU READY?" I asked her.

She most certainly was.

It was August 19, 2017. We were in a room at our friends' country home in Carp, Ontario, sequestered from the forty guests taking seats in the front yard. A white archway decorated with flowers awaited us.

Zoë wore a lovely champagne-coloured dress that went to her knees. Her chestnut hair framed her radiant face. She had on white shoes to match my dress, and I wore champagne shoes to match hers. Colour coordination among brides is *everything*.

She had dreamed of this moment for a long time. Our first wedding reflected not who she was but what society expected her to be. This wedding, this joyous do-over twenty years later, was her big day. She was able to wear a dress, be walked down the aisle and say vows all over again to the girl she had fallen in love with at a party so many years ago. But this time, she got to do it as herself.

This was her day, and she was going to enjoy every moment.

—

This was Zoë's day.

Hey, I just wanted twinkly lights and I got them, so I was happy.

After the ceremony, I sat under the big white tent in Leslie and Brad's backyard, watching my lovely bride dance the night away with our closest friends and family. I traced the circumference of my new wedding ring with my finger. We'd opted for matching silver ones this time; I had a feeling we'd be proudly wearing them every day. My vows to her had involved promising to watch Netflix in yoga pants with her for the rest of our lives. See? Romance isn't dead.

The guests were as much her loved ones as they were mine. My once-introverted spouse had morphed into a vivacious, engaging person who made friends easily. I loved watching this blossoming. I knew it was happening much later than she would have liked, but it was still beautiful.

I wish the girl from Peterborough had been able to live as that girl right from the start. I wish the first half of her life had been easier and more authentic. I wish she hadn't had to struggle for so long before finally being free. But then we never would have met. She likely would have never come to Ottawa. And even if she did, her life circumstances would have been different, and we probably would not have sat across from each other at that party. And even if, by chance, we had, I would never have allowed myself to fall in love with her. Not then, not there. I wasn't ready.

No, the circumstances needed to play out exactly as they had for us to find and hold onto each other. It has been an imperfect and at times dysfunctional love story. But it's *our* love story, and that love culminated in a remarkable family. While Zoë didn't get the life she deserved—the life Alexis now has a shot at—I hope that the deep love we share and the family we've built is still a nice consolation prize.

—

Lights beneath a white tent.

When Zoë was recovering from surgery, she took on most of the wedding planning. I told her this day was for her, so she could look and feel exactly how she wanted to, and I would be happy with anything.

She knew I was full of it.

She knew I wanted a white tent with lights strung up around it. I had only been talking about it for the past decade or so. She made sure to order them so I would smile extra wide on our special day too. That's my wife. She loves me far more than I deserve.

So there I was: hanging out in my perfect tent, under my perfect lights, watching my perfect bride. People made their way up to the deck—also filled with lights, obviously—to get food from the glorious potluck feast all our favourite people had put together. (It's not a lesbian celebration if it's not a potluck, you know.)

I used to think I loved our first wedding. I was wrong. I liked it. It was fun, but it didn't have the depth or meaning of this vow renewal. That day in 1997 felt more like an expectation; I was supposed to marry a guy, and Zoë was supposed to be one. This day, twenty years later, was a decision born from love and nothing else. The way it was supposed to be.

Earlier in the day, our dads had taken turns walking us down the aisle. Our moms gave speeches over dinner that made everyone cry. Little Jackson, now ten, was the handsome ring bearer.

Aerik, who was a baby at our first wedding, was our twenty-year-old officiant at this one, and he did an impressive job. Alexis, now a confident fourteen-year-old going through the right puberty and loving the changes to her body, was mixing tunes for us all night long in the DJ booth.

My brother Mike serenaded us with an adorably original love song after the speeches. Katie made sure her one-year-old, Alexa, was wearing her very best rainbow dress to be the flower girl at her aunts' wedding.

Many of our friends got involved too. Sarah, who had once made me coffee while I cried about my marriage being over, sang us down the aisle. Dani, a talented photographer I had met through the blogging community years before, took stunning photos of our ceremony. Jenn, a makeup artist who had given Zoë a makeover and tips when she first came out, made sure we looked incredible on our big day. Liliane provided a gorgeous cake—and the twinkly lights for the deck, of course, because she knows me well.

The last of our fears and worries, the ones that had built the walls we hid behind for most of our lives, dissipated that evening. If there was ever an example of true love between a couple, within a family and throughout a community, this was it. We were living it.

⁓

A few days later, we took the kids on a family honeymoon. We flew to Calgary, drove west through the Rockies and spent a few days in Vancouver before flying home. We connected with other trans people we knew along the way, including an up-and-coming politician in BC and a woman from Alberta who'd had surgery in Montreal on the same day as Zoë. We had lunch in Banff so I could introduce the women who had invited me to speak there to the family I had spoken so highly of. We held hands through the gay village in Vancouver, dipped our toes in the ocean, saw giant trees I had dreamed about visiting for a lifetime and came home with a pile of new memories.

The vow renewal and family honeymoon were our fresh start, our new beginning. Not long before, we were staring at a pile of rubble beneath our feet. Instead of walking away from it, we took the pieces and built something even more beautiful from them. My foundation—*our* foundation—is finally rock-solid.

I used to fear change, but now I welcome it. How do we grow without it? How do we get stronger without facing what we don't think we can possibly get through? I am a far better person today than I was before the night of February 25, 2014, when I stared in disbelief at an email from a frightened eleven-year-old. Since that day, she has taught me not only about the power of unconditional love, but a whole lot about myself too.

Alexis's courage changed not only her life but also the lives of both her moms. Because of her, Zoë was able to come out. And because of Zoë, I was able to do the same. We have all become better versions of ourselves, and our whole family is benefiting from that.

In 2017, I got a tattoo on my right forearm, the arm I shake everyone's hand with. It says "Lead with Love." It's a reminder to me that when we're trying to change the world, love must be our foundation. Hate is loud and violent, but it burns out quickly. Love is quieter and slower, but more resilient. It lingers longer and ultimately gets the job done. I've seen it work its magic in my own family, and I unquestionably believe in its power to do the same in society.

I will spend as long as it takes telling our story and fighting for families in which one or more people desperately need love, support and understanding. Families like ours. I'll know I don't have to fight anymore when I explain my family to others and no one bats an eye. When that happens—when folks just shrug like it's no big deal; when hate and judgment cease; when threats stop coming; when people truly see me, my wife, my daughter and our family as valid—I can hang up my advocacy hat for good. It will be a glorious day, but I don't think it will be anytime soon.

What I want the world to know more than anything is that yes, my family looks a little different these days, but not in the ways that really matter. We're a typical home filled with laughter, conversation, sibling rivalry, too much laundry, not enough vegetables and fights over who gets to pick the Friday-night movie.

And yeah, we have a couple of trans people and some gays. Who cares?

Some of the names and pronouns have changed, but the love remains the same.

SHE TOLD ME on the train.

My cellphone rang as I settled into my seat at Toronto's Union Station on a Friday afternoon. It was February 2018 and I was heading home from a business trip, tired from travel and meetings. But our case worker was calling, and I perked up immediately, hoping this was the news we had been waiting for.

"Hi, Amanda! I just wanted to let you and Zoë know that you've been approved for your kinship placement."

"That's wonderful!" I replied, a little too loudly for the quiet train car. "Ashley is coming over later. I can't wait to tell her! She's going to be so happy."

"I bet she is," the worker said. I could almost hear her smiling over the phone. "I'll be in touch after the weekend to talk about setting an official move-in date."

It was happening. Our family was about to go through another transition.

Two and a half years earlier, Alexis had been sitting at a school lunch table with her grade eight friends when she noticed a new girl scanning the room.

"You can sit with us," Alexis and her friends said, waving her over and making room.

Her name was Ashley, and she had just moved into a new foster-care home in the area. She and Alexis hit it off immediately, bonding over Minecraft, music and a love for the mall. They became inseparable. Alexis brought Ashley home to meet us, and she quickly became a regular, staying for dinner and weekend sleepovers.

Then, quite suddenly, she was gone.

Things hadn't worked out in her foster home, and with very little notice, she was uprooted from the school and Alexis, and placed in a group home across the city.

Alexis was gutted, but Ashley was used to it. By this point, she had been in and out of foster homes and the care of various family members for most of her life. She had been to fifteen different schools. Her norm was unpredictability.

One of the things she had learned was not to count on friendships; she had lost too many amid the upheaval. It was hard to stay in touch when you were young and always on the move, so she didn't try. For years, to save herself from the hurt of more goodbyes, she had avoided going to friends' houses and connecting with their lives outside of school. But she made an exception this time and stayed in touch with Alexis. She received permission from the group home to keep visiting her friend on weekends. We would drive across the city to pick her up on Saturday mornings and take her back in time for afternoon chores on Sundays.

When Ashley moved across the country to try living with a family member, the girls continued to keep in contact. When things didn't work out there and she flew back to Ottawa, the bright side was their reunion. But with so many failed attempts at stability, there was talk of her becoming a Crown ward. That would make the Province of Ontario her permanent caretaker until she aged out of the system.

"It looks like I'm out of options," fifteen-year-old Ashley told her friend.

Alexis didn't see it that way.

—

We didn't set out to add another teenager to our family. It happened in small, organic steps. In many ways, Ashley became a part of our family before we even considered the possibility. She was over as often as she could be, anchoring herself to the cheer and stability in our home. For all the changes we had gone through in the past few years, the connections between us had remained strong. She could feel it when she walked through the front door. Family could feel like this.

For Alexis, having a close friend was a new development. Before she came out, she was closed off and unable to connect with most other people her age. But now, our girl had a best friend. They chatted on the phone for hours, shared secrets and spent as much time together as possible. Zoë and I were excited to see their friendship grow. Moreover, we adored Ashley. Despite everything she had been through, she remained warm and optimistic.

Which is probably why, when Alexis sat us down and asked if Ashley could move in, it wasn't a difficult conversation.

"Aerik is moving out soon," she said. "And we'll have a spare bedroom. That could be her room."

With college under his belt and a full-time job in hand, twenty-one-year-old Aerik had plans to strike out on his own. I had hoped to turn his room into an office/guest bedroom, but this seemed like a far better use of the space.

Zoë and I had talked already about becoming foster parents, in particular to LGBTQ youth, since they're some of the most high-risk and underserved people. The timing of this potential placement was sooner than we had hoped, but it could work. And while Ashley didn't identify as LGBTQ, she was certainly an exceptional ally to a transgender girl we loved very much.

After a few weeks of assessments, records checks, references and home visits, I got that call on the train. The Children's Aid Society of Ottawa would be putting us forward to the courts as kinship caregivers to Ashley, which was the first step in her becoming a permanent family member.

⸺

I arrived back in Ottawa five hours after the social worker's call, my heart full, and made my way to the store for some important supplies to surprise Ashley with. When she walked through the door that evening for what she thought was an ordinary visit, she was greeted with balloons, a cake and a card welcoming her to the family. "This is like a dream," she said. "There's a saying between kids in foster care that once you reach about age ten, no one wants you anymore. You just bounce around until you age out. You'll never find a home. But look at this—I just found one!"

⸺

A few weeks later, Aerik moved into his own apartment. The morning after he left, I walked into his empty room, touched the walls where his posters used to be and shed a few tears. Kids grow up, and most of them eventually leave. That's a good thing. But I've learned that good isn't always easy.

I didn't have much time to mope, though—the room needed a make-over. Ashley was coming to live with us in four days. She had chosen a robin's-egg blue for her walls. "It's exciting to get to pick my room colour," she had said to me. "In most foster and group homes, you just get what you get, and it's usually pretty plain."

"But this isn't a foster home, honey," I said. "This is *your* home. *Your* room. We're going to make it special."

I spent the next three days not only painting but also adding some surprise touches, including a new duvet set in her favourite colours and some handmade wall art strategically placed to greet her as she opened the door. It said, "You are home."

We picked her up after school one day and carried the few bags she had filled with her possessions out to the car. She was excited, but still in disbelief. When she saw her new room, she began to cry.

"Welcome home," we said, hugging her.

And that is how we became a family of six.

Love grows.

ACKNOWLEDGMENTS

MY NAME MIGHT BE on this book, but it was by no means a one-woman process. I have a gratitude list a mile long, which I'll do my best to condense.

First and foremost, a profound thanks to the team at Penguin Random House Canada, including Scott Sellers and Nicole Winstanley, for believing in this project from the beginning and helping it come to life. A special note of thanks to Publishing Director Diane Turbide, who patiently worked her magic to help me shape our journey into one that could be told in book form. You've been a guide and a cheerleader—I couldn't have done this without you. And a heartfelt thank you to copyeditor Janice Weaver for sharp eyes and good questions.

Morgan Barnes, Richard Comeau and Jennifer Herman believed in this book before I did. Thank you giving me the push I needed to take this from a dream I was going to get to "someday" to something I actually did.

Cheers to my kids for putting up with a frazzled and often sleep-deprived mom, the long hours of me sequestered from the rest of the family, and for (mostly) adhering to my "I'm writing! Do NOT come in unless you're dying!" signs on the door. I love all four of you.

To my incredible wife, Zoë, for always insisting that writing *is* my "real job" and believing in me 110%, even when I didn't.

This whole book is a dedication to our love, but I'll say it again: I love you so much.

Mom, Dad, Katie, Charlie and Mike, thanks for always being there and for putting up with me as a teenager. I bet that was fun for you. To my in-laws, Liz and Cliff, knowing you love me like another daughter means the world to me.

Liliane Hajjar loved me through it—all of it—and she deserves a medal. My friends Jenn Annis and Shanon Ya-ya Page were my unofficial editors whenever I felt stuck. To our many friends who listened, learned, affirmed, and have celebrated with us ever since: I don't know what we'd do without you. Thanks for never letting us find out.

No writer is an island—although there are certainly times when many of us wish we could be on one. My thanks to friends Jen and Julia, who offered me the use of their family cottages so I could find solitude while hashing out the most challenging parts of this book.

My grade 10 writing teacher, Joyce Wagland, took a broken, angry teen aside after class and said, "You can write—*really* write. Did you know that?" and has believed in me ever since. Everyone needs that one great teacher. She was it for me.

To our community of Ottawa-Gatineau, your kindness and support has been paramount as we've navigated these changes. You began as my home by chance, you are now my home by choice.

And, finally, to every LGBTQ person who has lived their life out loud and proud before my time, to every trans activist who has fought for recognition, rights and respect, thank you. This book—and our family—wouldn't exist if not for you.